THE NEW JERSEY STATE
CONSTITUTION

**Reference Guides to the State Constitutions
of the United States**

This series includes a separate volume for each state constitution, analyzing its history and current status, providing a text of the constitution with a clause-by-clause commentary, a bibliography, a table of cases, and an index. A volume describing common themes and variations in state constitutional development and a final index volume to the preceding volumes are forthcoming.

THE NEW JERSEY STATE CONSTITUTION

A Reference Guide

Robert F. Williams

Foreword by Richard J. Hughes

REFERENCE GUIDES TO THE STATE CONSTITUTIONS OF THE UNITED STATES,
NUMBER 1

G. Alan Tarr, *Series Editor*

GREENWOOD PRESS

New York • Westport, Connecticut • London

For Alaine,
Sarah and Tyler

Library of Congress Cataloging-in-Publication Data

Williams, Robert F.
   The New Jersey State constitution : a reference guide / Robert F.
Williams ; foreword by Richard J. Hughes.
     p.   cm. — (Reference guides to the state constitutions of the
United States ; no. 1)
   Includes bibliographical references.
   ISBN 0–313–26245–4 (lib. bdg. : alk. paper)
   1. New Jersey—Constitutional law. 2. New Jersey—Constitutional
history. 3. New Jersey—Constitution. I. Title. II. Series.
KFN2202.W55   1990
342.749′029—dc20
[347.490229]   89–25912

British Library Cataloguing in Publication Data is available.

Library of Congress Catalog Card Number: 89–25912
ISBN: 0–313–26245–4

First published in 1990

Greenwood Press, Inc.
88 Post Road West, Westport, Connecticut 06881

Printed in the United States of America

The paper used in this book complies with the
Permanent Paper Standard issued by the National
Information Standards Organization (Z39.48-1984).

10 9 8 7 6 5 4 3 2 1

Contents

Contents

Series Foreword

In 1776, following the declaration of independence from England, the former colonies began to draft their own constitutions. Their handiwork attracted widespread interest, and draft constitutions circulated up and down the Atlantic seaboard, as constitution makers sought to benefit from the insights of their counterparts in sister states. In Europe, the new constitutions found a ready audience seeking enlightenment from the American experiments in self-government. Even the delegates to the Constitutional Convention of 1787, despite their reservations about the course of political developments in the states during the decade after independence, found much that was useful in the newly adopted constitutions. And when James Madison, fulfilling a pledge given during the ratification debates, drafted the Federal Bill of Rights, he found his model in the famous Declaration of Rights of the Virginia Constitution.

By the 1900s, however, few people would have looked to state constitutions for enlightenment. Instead, a familiar litany of complaints was heard whenever state constitutions were mentioned. State constitutions were too long and too detailed, combining basic principles with policy prescriptions and prohibitions that had no place in the fundamental law of a state. By including such provisions, it was argued, state constitutions deprived state governments of the flexibility they needed to respond effectively to changing circumstances. This—among other factors—encouraged political reformers to look to the federal government, which was not plagued by such constitutional constraints, thereby shifting the locus of political initiative away from the states. Meanwhile, civil libertarians concluded that state bills of rights, at least as interpreted by state courts, did not adequately protect rights and therefore looked to the federal courts and the federal Bill of Rights for redress. As power and responsibility shifted from the states to Washington, so too did the attention of scholars, the legal community, and the general public.

During the early 1970s, however, state constitutions were "rediscovered." The immediate impetus for this rediscovery was former President Richard Nixon's appointment of Warren Burger to succeed Earl Warren as Chief Justice of the United States Supreme Court. To civil libertarians, this appointment seemed to signal a decisive shift in the Supreme Court's jurisprudence, because Burger was expected to lead the Court away from the liberal activism that had characterized the Warren Court. They therefore sought ways to safeguard the gains they had achieved for defendants, racial minorities, and the poor during Warren's tenure from erosion by the Burger Court. In particular, they began to look to state bills of rights to secure the rights of defendants and to support other civil liberties claims that they advanced in state courts.

This "new judicial federalism," as it came to be called, quite quickly advanced beyond its initial concern to evade the mandates of the Burger Court. Indeed, less than two decades after it originated, it has become a nationwide phenomenon. For when judges and scholars turned their attention to state constitutions, they discovered an unsuspected richness. They found not only provisions that paralleled the federal Bill of Rights but also constitutional guarantees of the right to privacy and of gender equality, for example, that had no analogue in the U.S. Constitution. Careful examination of the text and history of state guarantees revealed important differences between even those provisions that most resembled federal guarantees and their federal counterparts. Looking beyond state declarations of rights, jurists and scholars discovered affirmative constitutional mandates to state governments to address such important policy concerns as education and housing. Taken altogether, these discoveries underlined the importance for the legal community of developing a better understanding of state constitutions.

Yet the renewed interest in state constitutions has not been limited to judges and lawyers. State constitutional reformers have renewed their efforts with notable success: since 1960, ten states have adopted new constitutions and several others have undertaken major constitutional revisions. These changes have usually resulted in more streamlined constitutions and more effective state governments. Also, in recent years political activists on both the left and the right have pursued their goals through state constitutional amendments, often enacted through the initiative process, under which policy proposals can be placed directly on the ballot for voters to endorse or reject. Scholars too have begun to rediscover how state constitutional history can illuminate changes in political thought and practice, providing a basis for theories about the dynamics of political change in America.

Robert Williams' fine study of the New Jersey Constitution is the first volume in the series, Reference Guides to the State Constitutions, which reflects this renewed interest in state constitutions and will contribute to our knowledge about them. Because the constitutional tradition of each state is distinctive, the volume begins with the history and development of the New Jersey Constitution. It then provides the full text of New Jersey's current constitution, with each section accompanied by commentary that explains the provision and traces its origins and its interpretation by the courts and other governmental bodies. For readers with a particular interest in a specific aspect of New Jersey constitutionalism, the book offers a bibliography of the most important sources dealing with the constitutional history and constitutional law of the state. Finally, the book concludes with a table of cases cited in the constitutional history and constitutional commentary, as well as a subject index.

G. Alan Tarr

Foreword

Professor Williams' scholarly tracing of constitutional development in New Jersey history is an important and refreshing discussion of the events that led from our first constitution of 1776 to the present day. His book prominently deals with the 1844 and 1947 Constitutions, under both of which I have had considerable experience. My early law practice was under the 1844 Constitution. On September 15, 1948, the effective date of the 1947 Constitution's Judicial Article, Article VI, I was sworn in as a County Court Judge under the new constitution. I later served two terms as governor in the 1960s and was Chief Justice of the New Jersey Supreme Court from 1973 to my retirement in August, 1979.

The 1947 New Jersey Constitution was the most exciting and wonderful thing that happened in my lifetime on the political level. My enthusiasm for the 1947 Constitution has roots in its history. As Professor Williams shows, for years prominent leaders in New Jersey had sought judicial reform, in view of the archaic court system provided by the 1844 Constitution, which was probably the worst in the country. That system divided courts and concepts of law and equity, to the disadvantage of litigants, and lacked any unifying administrative power. Its other failings gave rise to much hardship and the derisive term ''Jersey Justice.'' Authorities like Dean Roscoe Pound came here to urge court modernization upon our constitutional convention. A rare, once in a century, political miracle occurred when Govenor Al Driscoll and the Republicans and powerful Mayor Frank Hague and the Democrats, pushed and prodded by the reformers, agreed upon a new constitution. Upon submission to the voters, it was adopted by a large margin. Its centerpiece was the Judicial Article, which gave the new Supreme Court unprecedented administrative authority, vested in the Chief Justice, to control the administration of all courts in New Jersey. It gave rule-making flexibility to the Supreme Court, unequaled in any other jurisdiction, and insulated the court system from political interference. It accommodated easy transition of issues between courts of law and equity for expeditious consideration. These modern court system tools are unmatched in any other American jurisdiction. New Jersey's court system has become the envy of practitioners and scholars all over the country.

The 1947 Constitution, which is reproduced and analyzed in its entirety in this volume, replaced that of 1844, adopted in an agrarian state of 400,000 people. The 1844 Constitution remained in effect for more than a century, unmindful of the interim growth of business and industry, the move of corporate headquarters to the state, and the vast research and activity in electronic, drug, and chemical manufacture, accompanied by a growth of population to some five million (presently about seven million). The government under the 1844 Constitution was simply unequal to the task of governing the modern and complex state that New Jersey had become in the 1940s.

The other landmark feature of the 1947 Constitution was the establishment of a strong governor, probably the strongest in the nation, who is the only statewide elected official. Through an increase in the governor's veto, appointment and other powers, as well as extending the term and permitting succession, the new constitution created the possibility of a strong, central executive leader for New Jersey. That is what our governors have been, both through the exercise of formal and informal powers. Of course, legislative power, particularly the power of the Senate, is formidable, even in the face of these new gubernatorial powers.

Adoption of the constitution in 1947, of course, did not put an end to constitutional developments in New Jersey. As the state's political institutions have responded to emerging problems, the constitution has guided their responses. New controversies have also arisen under the constitution, which can be resolved only through its interpretation by the judiciary or by other branches of the state's government. Finally, New Jersey's voters have on several occasions amended the constitution. These developments make Professor Williams' constitutional commentary, which examines the interpretation of each constitutional provision in the period since 1947, essential reading for all who seek to understand New Jersey's constitution.

I have been asked many times what flaws are in the 1947 Constitution, and what changes I would recommend in the 1947 Constitution. I do not like things to change when they are working well, and I frankly do not see any flaws in the Constitution of New Jersey.

Richard J. Hughes

Introduction

New Jersey's well-known and much envied constitution of 1947 is now more than forty years old. Just after its twentieth anniversary, two knowledgeable observers concluded: "the New Jersey constitution is strictly a basic constitutional document, not a code of laws. . . . We venture to guess that until or unless New Jersey's constitution is seriously blemished by the accumulation of restrictive amendments, there will be no overpowering demand for general revision."[1] The same conclusions may be reached today, after well over two centuries of experience in New Jersey with state constitutionalism. The state's constitutional structure, however, has not always been the subject of such praise.

A study of a state's constitutional development can provide important insight into the broader issues of that state's political, economic, and social growth. In this sense, state constitutions have been referred to as "a mine of instruction for the natural history of democratic communities," and as a "cinematoscope of the times."[2] This is true in New Jersey, although here, as in all states, much that has taken place in the evolution of governmental and political power is not reflected in the state constitution.

Although a state's constitutional development since Independence cannot be completely understood without reference to the state's earlier colonial history, a study such as this must exclude a treatment of that era. Fortunately, New Jersey's rich colonial history, including its colonial constitutional history, has been treated elsewhere. This volume treats New Jersey's constitutional development since statehood in 1776, and provides a section-by-section analysis of its current constitution.

NOTES

1. John E. Bebout and Joseph Harrison, "The Working of the New Jersey Constitution," *William and Mary Law Review* 10 (1968):338, 357.

2. James Bryce, *The American Commonwealth*, 2d ed., rev. (1891), 1:434; James Quale Dealey, *Growth of American State Constitutions* (1915; reprint, New York: DaCapo, 1972), 2. Justice Vincent S. Haneman's concurring opinion in Jackman v. Bodine, 43 N.J. 453, 479, 205 A.2d 713, 727 (1964) contains an excellent judicial sketch of New Jersey's constitutional development.

Part I

The Constitutional History of
New Jersey

CONSTITUTION OF 1776

We Shall Have A Republick Established By The End Of The Week

New Jersey's 1776 Constitution, the fourth state constitution to be adopted that year is not one of the well-known early state constitutions. Those who study early state constitutions focus, rather, on the better-known examples of this era: Virginia (1776), Pennsylvania (1776), and Massachusetts (1780). A scholar of the early state constitutions concluded that in New Jersey, by contrast to other states, the 1776 Constitution was adopted with little controversy.[1]

The 1776 Constitution was drafted by a committee of the revolutionary Provincial Congress, meeting in Burlington, not by a convention elected specially for the purpose of drafting a constitution. On June 21, 1776, the congress resolved, by a vote of 54 to 3, "that a government be formed for regulating the internal policy of this Colony." On June 24 a ten-man committee was formed and within two days had a working draft. Also on June 24 petitions were received from Middletown and Freehold, Monmouth County, "praying that this Congress would immediately establish such mode of government as shall be equal to the exigencies of this Colony."

On July 2, after the departure of nearly half of the delegates for unknown reasons, the constitution was adopted by a vote of 26 to 9. There was no popular ratification of this constitution, but a thousand copies were printed and distributed.

The primary drafter was apparently Jonathan Dickinson Sergeant, who had been a delegate to the Continental Congress in Philadelphia, where he met John

Adams.[2] Sergeant asked Adams for a copy of his letter about how the new state constitutions should be structured. This letter by John Adams was later published as his famous *Thoughts on Government*. As Sergeant returned to New Jersey from the Continental Congress in Philadelphia, possibly carrying a draft constitution, he wrote back to Samuel Adams: "We shall have a Republick established by the end of the week."[3]

Constitution making in New Jersey took place in war time. Cecilia Kenyon reminds us that "every member of the state assemblies or conventions that drafted constitutions was publicly committing himself to the Revolution and therefore placing his life in jeopardy should the Revolution fail."[4] This may make it more understandable that Article 23 of New Jersey's first constitution concluded with the following caveat:

Provided always, and it is the true Intent and Meaning of this Congress, that if Reconciliation between Great Britain and these Colonies should take place, and the latter be again taken under the Protection and Government of the Crown of Great Britain, this Charter shall be null and void, otherwise to remain firm and inviolable.[5]

This provision was apparently the subject of the most heated debates over the constitution, but remained in the final version.

In April 1776, in defending the much criticized British Constitution, Chief Justice Frederick Smyth, who was a British official and opponent of independence, had warned of the dangers of a "new fangled Ideal Mode of Government."[6] The constitution that emerged four months later was, rather than "new fangled," a fairly close replication of New Jersey's colonial structure of government.[7] It reflected the general revolutionary political philosophy of legislative supremacy and is probably one of the most extreme examples of "legislative omnipotence."[8] New Jersey did not, however, adopt the radically democratic constitutional ideas (one-house legislature, no checks and balances, etc.) that were current in Pennsylvania and which led to that state's "ultra-democratic" constitution of September 1776.

New Jersey's brief 1776 Constitution contained no separate Bill of Rights. About half of the first state constitutions contained bills of rights, with those in Virginia (1776) and Massachusetts (1780) being the most well known. This omission provided one of the major arguments finally leading to the adoption of the New Jersey Constitution of 1844. Still, although the 1776 document did not contain a Declaration of Rights, it included some important rights with the other structural provisions contained in the constitution.[9] For example, Article 4 provided "all Inhabitants of this Colony of full Age, who are worth Fifty Pounds . . . shall be entitled to vote." This was an important expression of the right to popular participation in government and supported a statutory grant of voting rights to blacks and women in New Jersey from 1790 until 1807, when it was repealed.[10] No challenge seems to have been made at the time to the withdrawal of these early, important voting rights, which had been exercised by

New Jerseyites generations before such rights were protected by other state constitutions or by the federal constitution.

To a certain extent, the general expansion of participation in government (not necessarily voting by blacks and women) was the logical extension of the wide participation in the events leading up to the Revolution. As Larry Gerlach has noted:

The new politics, intended primarily to broaden the base of support for extralegal protest activities, simultaneously heightened public awareness of the major issues of the day and brought many people into the political process whom the law excluded from meaningful participation in regular provincial politics. In a word, it was an impetus to democratic politics.[11]

In fact, the qualifications for voting in the elections for the extralegal Provincial Congress that promulgated the constitution were very similar to those contained in the constitution itself. These factors fit into and support the Revolutionary concept of legislative supremacy where a broadly representative legislature represents the popular will with little interference from the other branches of government. Legislative politics in New Jersey after 1776 formed the basis for the emergence of parties as we know them. Jackson Turner Main concluded that after 1776 two basic political groups emerged:

One drew its principal strength from West Jersey. . . . During the war, its members were less anxious to pursue vigorous measures. On various occasions they opposed calling out the militia and providing for their pay in times of emergency, fought the grant of extraordinary power to the executive, voted against tax increases and various government expenditures, opposed heavy penalties for trading with the enemy, negatived antimonopoly bills and price controls, defended newspaper criticism of the government, seemed a little more sympathetic with loyalists, and were much less anxious to support Congress than were their political opposites. With peace they began to shift ground and adapt to new circumstances. They now became eager to uphold the government and concentrate power in Congress, they approved government expenses, the collection of taxes, and permanent salaries, they defended the rights of large landowners and of creditors, and fought paper money. On all of these issues an equally determined group of delegates, primarily from East Jersey, supported opposite policies.[12]

Article 16 provided that "Criminals shall be admitted to the same Privileges of Witnesses and Counsel, as their Prosecutors are or shall be entitled to." Articles 18 and 19 reflected early notions of religious freedom ("worshipping Almighty God in a manner agreeable to the Dictates of his own Conscience"), prohibition of "Establishment of any one religious Sect . . . in preference to another," and rights against discrimination for *protestants*. Article 22 declared that the "Common Law of England . . . shall still remain in Force . . . such Parts only expected as are repugnant to the Rights and Privileges contained in this Charter," and that "the inestimable Right of Trial by Jury shall remain confirmed . . . without Repeal for ever."

In a very interesting provision, Article 23 required an oath of persons elected to the legislature, promising not to agree to any law "that shall annul or repeal" the requirement of annual legislative elections or the religious freedom or jury trial provisions. Because the constitution had been promulgated by a legislative body, it was presumably subject to amendment by that same body. For example, in 1777 the legislature circumvented Article 15 of the constitution, which required writs and commissions to run in the name of the *Colony* of New Jersey, in a statute substituting the word "State" for "Colony."[13] New Jersey's provision, although using the indirect form of an oath, seems to be the first state constitutional statement placing "the most important portion [of the constitution] beyond amendment."[14]

The jury trial provision gave rise to one of the few and possibly the earliest of the pre-Marbury v. Madison examples of judicial review in Holmes v. Walton (1780).[15] This New Jersey case involved a successful challenge to a six-man jury provision contained in a statute concerning trade with the British. The legislature acquiesced and amended the act to include the twelve-man jury required by common law. Edward S. Corwin stated that the Holmes case was the initial example of judicial review after Independence.[16]

The constitutional text contained no specific protection for vested rights in property, that is, the notion that government could not unreasonably interfere with ownership and other interests in property. Apparently, however, as Charles Erdman concluded, the New Jersey courts began to recognize this limitation on legislative power without any textual basis in the constitution.[17]

The structure of government contained in the constitution gave little recognition to what we now refer to as separation of powers. This drew specific criticism a little over a decade later from James Madison in *The Federalist*, Number Forty-Seven. As noted earlier, the annually elected bicameral legislature (Art. 3), made up of a legislative council (the "upper house" and precursor to the senate) and assembly, dominated the government. The two houses, sitting in "joint meeting" appointed most state and local administrative and judicial officials. The legislature annually elected "some fit Person within the Colony" to be governor (Art. 7). The governor had no veto power, nor did he have power of appointment. He was, however, to serve as chancellor (Art. 8)—a requirement that worked to guarantee that all New Jersey governors between 1776 and 1844 were lawyers![18]

Legislative election of the governor seems to have had important effects on party politics in New Jersey. In the absence of a chief executive who was elected in a statewide election, there was no New Jersey focal point for political parties. In this vacuum the focus shifted to national candidates and local legislative races.[19]

However, legislative election did not preclude the forceful exercise of gubernatorial power. The lack of formal executive powers in the constitution reflected a situation common in the early state constitutions. New Jersey's first governor, William Livingston, elected after an initial tie vote in the legislature with Richard Stockton, was a major force in government during the war years.[20] He set the legislative agenda in his addresses to the legislature and exercised bold and decisive executive and military leadership.

The constitution provided for a clearly dependent judiciary. Article 1 provided that "the Government of this Province shall be vested in a Governor, Legislative Council, and General Assembly." The judiciary was not even named as a branch. The early view was that the judiciary was a part of the executive branch, and that, as with the executive, judges should be named by the legislature. Therefore, Article 12 provided that judges be selected by the legislature for limited terms— a mechanism creating obvious dependence. On this subject a New York newspaper noted that "there is not now in New Jersey, one single tribunal entrusted with the decision of legal controversies, which can be said to possess the qualifications of independence and impartiality: they all of them are shackled by party, or influenced by dependence."[21]

The governor and Legislative Council served as the "Court of Appeals in the Last Resort" (Art. 9). This often provided a political review of legal decisions rendered by the Supreme Court (Art. 12), leading to Chief Justice Joseph C. Hornblower's comment at the 1844 Constitutional Convention that the Court of Appeals had "long since been christened by eminent counsel, not the Court for the correction of Errors but the Court of high errors!"[22]

Article 3 provided for equal representation for each county in the upper house, or Legislative Council, regardless of population. This provision dominated state constitutional debates in New Jersey for nearly two centuries and served as a barrier to state constitutional change because the small counties feared change would lead to the loss of their equal voice in the upper house.

Somehow, however, New Jersey managed to operate under its brief, temporary, and obviously flawed constitution for sixty-eight years until it was replaced by the 1844 Constitution. In an 1802 case challenging the legitimacy of the 1776 Constitution, which had never been submitted to the people for ratification, Justice Andrew Kirkpatrick observed:

Whatever might be said upon theoretical principles, considering that the constitution was framed by a convention never delegated for that purpose, and therefore never vested with competent authority therefore; and considering also that it was not even by that convention intended or meant to be a perpetual law, but only to answer the pressing exigency of the times, as is manifest from its being made before the declaration of independence, as well as from many badges of colonial distinction which it still wears upon it; yet, notwithstanding these considerations, it has by general consent been received, and used ever since as the legitimate constitution of the state.

Without looking, therefore, into the spuriousness of its origin, we must receive and treat it as such, until the people shall think proper to lay it aside, and to establish a better in its place.[23]

When, in 1844, the people adopted a revised constitution, it lasted more than a century before being replaced by the 1947 New Jersey Constitution. The roots of New Jersey constitutionalism, however, are traceable to the 1776 Constitution and its colonial antecedents.

CONSTITUTION OF 1844

The constitutional experiments in the states between 1776 and 1791 and continuing thereafter produced a great accumulation of constitutional experience and knowledge, particularly with respect to the function of separation of powers and checks and balances in republican governments. There was an important wave of constitutional revision in other states in the 1820s. New Jersey, however, failed to avail itself of the lessons of this constitutional experience at the state and federal levels until its 1844 Constitutional Convention.

The 1776 Constitution had addressed itself to the possibility of reconciliation with Britain but contained no mechanism for change in the event such reconciliation did not take place. Advances in constitutional theory since 1776 had divested the legislature of its earlier assumed power, acquiesced in by the people, to promulgate and amend a constitution itself. A constitution's paramount status, subject to change only by the people, was better understood after 1800. Further, social and economic conditions had not changed enough to demand a more refined government. All of these factors operated to frustrate constitutional change.

New Jersey's first constitution was criticized for its lack of a separate bill of rights. Some argued this was unnecessary because English common law, adopted in New Jersey, protected most rights. Others defended the absence of a bill of rights by arguing that in the attempt to write a declaration of rights, certain important protections might be left out. An even more important criticism of the constitution, however, was based on the maturing understanding of the separation of powers doctrine. William Griffith, a well-known lawyer from Burlington, wrote a series of fifty-three articles in the *New Jersey Gazette* in 1798 under the name "Eumenes," meaning "well-disposed." These articles were designed to persuade the legislature to call a constitutional convention, a matter it began considering seriously in the late 1790s. Griffith's major criticism was the absence of an effective separation of powers, with particular emphasis on the dominance of the legislative branch, which appointed the governor and judges, as well as most local officials. This appointment power came to overshadow and adversely affect the process of passing legislation. Griffith also criticized the upper house, which sat as a court of last resort. As governor earlier in the decade, William Patterson had made similar observations, and many of these same criticisms surfaced in the 1844 convention.

Despite the telling criticisms of the 1776 Constitution by constitutional theorists, the citizens of New Jersey were not convinced that the practical consequences for their lives were serious enough to risk changes in the existing government structure. One journalist in 1802 wrote that despite the imperfections in the constitution "I do not know but that the people of this State, generally, live as quiet and as happy under it, as the people of those States who have revised and amended theirs.''[24] New Jersey also did not witness the class and political conflicts between interior farming interests and coastal commercial interests that caused pressure for constitutional change in other states during the first quarter of the nineteenth century.[25]

Legislative efforts to call a constitutional convention were defeated three times between 1790 and 1798. In 1800 the people voted ''no'' on the question of whether a constitutional convention should be called. In 1819 the voters overwhelmingly rejected an amendment to change the date of legislative elections, the merits of which were noncontroversial. In 1817 a memorial submitted by a number of prominent citizens requesting a constitutional convention received no legislative or even newspaper support.[26]

Finally, after the economic Panic of 1837 and the onset of the Industrial Revolution, when the theoretical defects in the 1776 Constitution began to cause practical problems, the movement for constitutional reform gained momentum.[27] By 1844 New Jersey's constitution was the oldest written constitution in existence. Governor Pennington's 1840 message to the legislature, describing from personal experience the conflict between the office of governor and chancellor, ''sounded the death-knell of the Constitution of 1776.''[28]

There was no referendum on whether to call a constitutional convention. The legislature's 1844 act provided for the election of delegates by a wider electorate than that specified in the 1776 Constitution and a strict timetable for action.[29] In short order and with a minimum of party strife, New Jersey had a new constitution that was ratified overwhelmingly by the voters. The relatively brief 1844 Constitution, although not a radical departure from the earlier constitution, cured many of its most obvious defects. The fifty-eight delegates meeting in Trenton, most of whom had direct experience in state or local government, made use of the experience of the past sixty-eight years and the many available constitutional models.

A separate bill of rights, the basis of today's Article I, was added in 1844. It is important to note that it was placed at the *beginning* of the constitution, by contrast to the federal Constitution, where the Bill of Rights is appended at the end as amendments. This distinction is important, as Daniel Elazar has observed: ''Most immediately, their place at the beginning of the constitution is intended to announce that the protection of rights is the first task of government, indeed, its *raison d'être*.''[30] Of course, New Jersey's 1776 Constitution had not been set up this way.

The right of suffrage was restricted so as to exclude blacks and women and also ''paupers,'' but broadened so as to eliminate property requirements for voting by white males.[31] The legislative council was renamed the senate, the term of office was extended from one to three years, but equal representation for counties was retained. The weak 1776 reapportionment provision for the assembly, based on population, was strengthened and most of the legislature's appointment powers were removed.[32] The governor became an elected officer (a representative of the people), with veto power and a three-year term, and the duties of chancellor were removed from the office. However, he could not succeed himself, a problem to which Woodrow Wilson pointed years later, commenting that everyone else in government could "smile at the coming and going of governors . . . as upon things ephemeral, which passed and were soon enough got rid of if you but sat tight and waited."[33] The veto was "weak," in that it could be overridden by only a majority vote, but it was an important new power. Most judges and other officials were no longer appointed by the joint meeting of the legislature but by the governor. The Court of Appeals was re-constituted as the Court of Errors and Appeals, made up of the chancellor, supreme court justices, and six appointed lay judges. Finally, the constitution set forth a mechanism for amendments, albeit a very cumbersome one, patterned on the Pennsylvania constitution, requiring passage by two legislative sessions (there were annual assembly elections) and prohibiting amendments from being submitted more often than once in five years. The debates on the amendment process were dominated by a desire not to permit hasty "agitation" for consti-tutional change, with the equal representation of counties in the senate surfacing over and over as the provision most likely to be changed.[34]

The 1844 Constitution reflected much of the accumulated dissatisfaction with the performance of the dominant legislative branch. A Legislative Council report noted that New Jersey was the only state to place the appointing power in the legislature, causing evil influence on legislation. A delegate at the 1844 con-vention complained that therefore "a divorce bill, an office and railroad acts might all be tied up together in one bargain bundle." A complementary concern was the weak governor, which, according to an 1840 assembly judiciary com-mittee report, had less power than any other governor.

The new constitution prohibited special legislation for internal improvements and prohibited the legislature from creating debt over $100,000 without a majority vote of the electors. There was clear recognition of problems in other states leading to the Panic of 1837. The new requirement that "every law shall embrace but one object and that shall be expressed in the title" seemed to be drawn directly from colonial times—Queen Anne's 1702 Instructions to Lord Corn-bury.[35] Interestingly, the governor's new veto power was not utilized until 1851 by Governor George F. Fort, but in following years was used to block a number of special bills granting corporate charters.[36]

The advent of a Bill of Rights stimulated litigation almost immediately. Article I, paragraph 1 provided: "All men are by nature free and independent." The legislature had passed a bill in 1804 freeing the children of slaves born in the state, but apprenticing them to their mothers' masters until twenty-one for females and twenty-five for males. Immediately after the adoption of the 1844 Consti-tution, abolitionists initiated litigation under Article I, paragraph 1, seeking a determination that slavery was unconstitutional in New Jersey. Alvan Stewart, a prominent New York abolitionist, sought habeas corpus on behalf of two clients: a slave born before the 1804 law was enacted, and a child of a slave born after the law took effect.[37] In the 1845 decision in State v. Post, however, the New Jersey Supreme Court held that the new constitution did not abolish slavery. Justice James S. Nevius concluded that

had the convention intended to abolish slavery and domestic relations, well known to exist in this state and to be established by law, and to divest the master of his right of property in his slave . . . no one can doubt that it would have adopted some clear and definite provision to effect it, and not to have left so important and grave a question . . . to depend upon the doubtful construction of an indefinite abstract political proposition.

Justice Joseph F. Randolph pointed to the convention's decision not to adopt the original draft version—"all men are born equally free and independent"— to justify a similar conclusion.[38]

THE 1873 CONSTITUTIONAL COMMISSION

Despite important reforms, the 1844 New Jersey Constitution "made only a modest step toward transforming its government."[39] Quite soon after the adoption of the 1844 Constitution, proposals for further constitutional change began to surface. The focus of these proposals was on the structure and functioning of the court system, together with the process of selecting judges. Special commissions were appointed in 1852 and 1854 to investigate these matters, but their recommendations were rejected by the legislature.[40]

On the legislative front, the practice of special or local legislation (laws concerning only a few persons, business entities, or localities) continued despite some gubernatorial vetoes and public criticisms. In his 1873 address to the legislature, Governor Joel Parker suggested a constitutional convention or commission to recommend amendments and reported that the general laws passed at the 1872 session occupied about 100 pages, while the special and private laws consumed 1,250 pages.[41] Fearful of a convention it could not control, the legislature did not pass legislation calling for a constitutional convention, but adopted a resolution on the last day of its 1873 session giving the governor the power to appoint, with advice and consent of the senate, a commission that would recommend state constitutional amendments to the next legislative session.[42] Thus, the cumbersome amendment procedure of the 1844 Constitution was preserved. Governor Parker, concluding that "it is important that amendments to the constitution should be prepared and ready to be submitted for consideration at the opening of the next session of the legislature," called the senate back into special session to confirm his nominations to the fourteen-member commission.[43] After confirmation, he convened the commission in the senate chamber in Trenton on May 8, 1873.

After convening, the constitutional commission elected its officers, broke down into four committees, and proceeded to consider the entire range of possible constitutional changes. The president of the commission was John C. Ten Eyck, who had served in the 1844 Constitutional Convention. The commission met on eighteen separate days between July 8 and November 18, 1873, after which it submitted its recommended state constitutional changes to the legislature.

The commission followed Governor Parker's recommendation and proposed a long series of specific limits on private, local, and special laws, which were adopted after being approved by the legislature. Most other recommendations were aimed at the legislative branch, with the most well known of those approved by the legislature and adopted by the people, including the mandate that the legislature provide for a "thorough and efficient system of free public schools," the item veto for the governor, the requirement that property be assessed for taxation "under general laws and by uniform rules, according to its true value," and the transfer from the legislature to the governor of the power to appoint trial judges. Proposals such as one to strengthen the governor's veto power by requiring a two-thirds vote of the legislature for override and another to limit the legislature's power to cap damages were recommended by the commission, but not submitted by the legislature to the voters. Other proposals, such as to abolish equal representation for counties in the senate, to provide for elected judges, and to move to legislative sessions only every two years, were debated in the commission but not recommended to the legislature.

In his annual address to the legislature, Governor Parker lauded the commission's work: "Seldom has a deliberative body convened in which so little local prejudice or partizan [sic] feeling existed, or in which greater patriotism, wisdom and discretion were displayed." He told the legislature it was about to engage in "the most important work legislators can be called upon to do."[44]

The years 1873–75 saw major revisions in the New Jersey Constitution. All twenty-eight amendments submitted by the legislature were approved by the voters in a special election in 1875. During 1873 and 1874 matters relating to the whole range of state constitutional concerns, although with a special focus on the legislative branch, were fully debated in both the constitutional commission and the legislature. The two-year period stands behind only three others in significance for state constitutional development in New Jersey: 1776, 1844, and 1947. In fact, it could be argued that in 1875 the New Jersey Constitution was so significantly revised that we should think of the "1875 New Jersey Constitution" as a fourth state constitution. This is particularly true in light of New Jersey's otherwise rare changes in its constitutional text. Furthermore, as John Bebout observed in 1942, the "1875 amendments necessarily entailed a tremendous increase in judicial review of legislation. Since 1875 over half of the more than 300 legislative acts invalidated by the courts were nullified because of the 1875 amendments."[45]

Reformers continued to call for the elimination of equal representation of counties in the senate. The following 1873 editorial from the *Newark Daily Advertiser* illustrated the nature of the problem:

The pine-barrens have beaten the populace. Ten gentlemen, representing the wealth, power honour and good sense of the State of New Jersey, representing also the bulk of its population and its true will and purpose, yesterday voted for a competing railroad between New York and Philadelphia. Eleven other men, whose title is Senator, representing an innumerable host of stunted pines, growing on sand-barrens, voted the bill down . . . You can't make pine trees vote nor endow them with a conscience.

CONSTITUTIONAL CHANGE FROM 1875 TO 1940

Only six years after adoption of the 1875 amendments, the legislature again provided for a constitutional commission in 1881. The commission met and submitted fairly wide-ranging recommendations to the 1882 legislature, but no constitutional amendments were proposed or adopted as a result of the commission's labors.[46]

In an important 1893 case interpreting the 1844 Constitution, the Supreme Court struck down the use of single-member assembly districts, thereby permitting only the use of at-large elections for the members of the assembly from each county (State v. Wrightson). This approach was upheld by the Court of Errors and Appeals in 1906 (Smith v. Baker).

In 1897 two legislatively proposed amendments were adopted by the voters. One amendment prohibited the governor from making appointments to office during senate recesses. The other amendment extended the 1844 Constitution's prohibition on lotteries and the sale of lottery tickets to prohibit gambling generally. This amendment, adopted in response to the strong influence in the legislature by race track interests, began the long New Jersey practice of regulating gambling in the constitution, which continues today. The courts rejected a challenge to the process by which the antigambling amendment was submitted to the voters (Bott v. Secretary of State).

At the same time these amendments were adopted, a third, providing for women's suffrage, was rejected by the voters. After 1897 efforts to obtain the vote for women moved to the courts, under the leadership of Mary Philbrook, the first woman lawyer in New Jersey. She relied on the 1776 Constitution, which had granted the vote to "inhabitants," without regard to sex. Philbrook argued that the 1844 Constitution's limitation of the franchise to "white males" was invalid because women were neither permitted to vote for delegates to the 1844 convention nor to vote on ratification of the 1844 Constitution. This novel argument was rejected in 1912 (Carpenter v. Cornish).[47]

A new movement was then begun to adopt a women's suffrage amendment to the state constitution. After successful passage through the legislature in two sessions, the presiding officers did not properly advertise the amendment. It was therefore reintroduced, passed, properly advertised, but defeated in 1915.[48] At the same election, probably in the wake of votes against women's suffrage, an amendment that would have liberalized the procedure for amending the state constitution by eliminating the requirement of a special election was also defeated. Thus, New Jersey remained subject to "constitutional rigidity."[49]

This difficulty in achieving constitutional change through the mechanism set forth in the 1844 Constitution began to lead to the serious consideration of a dramatic alternative—the constitutional convention—the very source of the 1844 Constitution itself. In 1913 Governor Woodrow Wilson told the legislature: "There are other things we have outgrown. The constitution of the State needs reconsideration in a score of parts, some of them of the first consequence. . . . I urge upon you very earnestly indeed the need and demand for a constitutional convention."[50] A range of arguments, including one that a convention was illegal because not authorized in the 1844 constitution, and the ever-present fear of elimination of equal representation for counties in the senate, led to defeat of the convention bill in 1913. The debate concerning the legality of a constitutional convention continued into the 1940s.[51]

In 1927 a constitutional amendment added what now appears in slightly altered form as Article IV, Section VI, paragraph 2, of the New Jersey Constitution, which authorized the legislature, by general law to permit municipalities to enact zoning ordinances. This amendment was the only one to be adopted in 1927 during a flurry of partisan opposition to several other amendments on the ballot, including another one to liberalize the amendment process itself.[52] The 1927 zoning amendment was ratified to overcome decisions by the New Jersey courts holding that, under both the state and federal constitutions, the legislature did not have the power to delegate the authority to zone to municipalities (Ignaciunas v.Town of Nutley; Krumgold & Sons v. Mayor and Aldermen of Jersey City). Once the United States Supreme Court ruled in 1926, however, that municipal zoning did not violate the *federal* constitution (Euclid v. Ambler Realty Co.), the way was cleared for local zoning to be authorized by an amendment to the *state* constitution. Interestingly, when called on to analyze the power apparently granted by the zoning amendment, the New Jersey Supreme Court has characterized it as a basic attribute of police power, no greater than the basic power always possessed by the state legislature (Roselle v. Wright).

In 1930 the Court of Errors and Appeals, in a case involving the alleged illegal activities of Jersey City mayor Frank Hague, interpreted the legislature's constitutional power to investigate in a narrow manner (In re Hague). The court concluded that a joint session of the legislature could not punish Hague for contempt, based on his refusal to answer questions after being subpoenaed before it, because it was attempting to investigate violations of the criminal laws, which was the province of the judiciary where a defendant is protected against self-incrimination. This holding became the subject of constitutional revision throughout the 1940s, culminating in the current provision in Article IV, Section V, paragraph 2, permitting the legislature to appoint a commission or committee to "aid or assist it in performing its functions."

In 1939 voters amended the 1897 prohibition on gambling to permit pari-mutuel betting on horse racing, conditioned on significant revenues going to the state. Interestingly, it was the issue of horse racing that led to the 1897 state constitutional gambling ban.

THE 1947 CONSTITUTION

The movement that culminated in the adoption of New Jersey's "model" Constitution of 1947 actually began in earnest in 1940. From that date until 1947, a succession of three governors made constitutional reform a high priority in their administrations. Governors Charles Edison, Walter E. Edge, and Alfred E. Driscoll, each unable to succeed himself, saw the need for major revisions in the state's century-old constitution if New Jersey was going to face up to the modern problems of postwar state governments. During this period, from 1940 to 1947, suggestions for substantive change in the constitution were enmeshed in both the restrictive process for constitutional change and in broader questions of partisan politics. Also during this period, what had earlier been a hypothetical question—the legality of a constitutional convention despite the lack of any authorizing provision in the 1844 Constitution—became a practical and crucial matter for constitutional revision.

Governor Edison made constitutional revision a key focus of his 1940 campaign and his 1941 inaugural address, calling for a constitutional convention.[53] Edison emphasized the need for a stronger governor, with control over a streamlined executive branch and a meaningful veto, elimination of equal representation for counties in the senate, a simpler method of constitutional amendment, and a modernized court system. These issues became the central themes of the reformers through the long efforts leading to the 1947 Constitution, and most of them are reflected in New Jersey's current constitution.

The legislature, however, still feared a constitutional convention. No convention bill was adopted and instead, as the realities of war settled on the state and nation, the legislature in 1941 created another constitutional commission to suggest constitutional changes "to provide for the more effective working of present-day representative processes." The commission was continued and reconstituted in 1942 and became known as the Hendrickson Commission, after its chair, Senator Robert C. Hendrickson. The commission first sought an extension of time for its product, and then embarked on drafting an entirely new constitution.[54] The commission, with relatively little outside influence, proceeded to draft a brief, modern constitution, which formed a model for the state constitutional dialogue of the next five years.[55] This draft addressed many of the concerns outlined by Governor Edison.

The commission submitted its draft to the legislature with a request that the cumbersome amendment procedure of the 1844 Constitution be bypassed by a September primary vote of the electors on whether a new constitution could be submitted at the November 1942 general election. The legislature formed a joint committee to hold public hearings on the various proposals and recommendations for change in the constitution made by the commission. The joint committee held nine days of public hearings, which was the first major public discussion of state constitutional revision in New Jersey since 1875.[56] Its published *Pro-*

ceedings reflect the entire range of opinion about substantive revisions, as well as the existing procedural options for constitutional change. Governor Edison appeared personally, endorsing the Hendrickson Commission Report and Draft Constitution. He invoked Woodrow Wilson's 1913 call for state constitutional revision and asked the committee to hear him "impersonally as the voice of the many Governors who have tried, in spite of great handicaps, to serve the people under the 1844 Constitution." Edison noted that over half of the twenty governors elected since the 1875 revisions had gone on record for changes in the 1844 Constitution. He then praised the Hendrickson Commission report "as a landmark in the history of constitutional progress in New Jersey."[57]

At the end of the public hearings, however, the opponents of constitutional revision advanced an important and decisive argument: that it was unfair to proceed with state constitutional revision while so many New Jersey men were away fighting the war. The committee agreed, noting this fairness issue in its September 1942 report back to the legislature recommending "that no further action for change in the New Jersey State Constitution be taken until after the termination of the present war."[58]

However, the legislature did not wait. The two dissenting members of the Joint Legislative Committee assumed positions of leadership for the 1943 session and successfully pushed a bill that would ask the voters to vote on whether the 1944 legislature should be authorized to draft a new constitution, but not be permitted to change the Bill of Rights or the form of legislative representation. With the help of gubernatorial candidate Walter Edge, the bill passed and the voters approved the referendum authorizing the 1944 legislature to act as a limited constitutional convention.[59]

In Governor Edison's final message to the legislature in 1944, he noted proudly that "the progress we have made toward constitutional revision is by far the most important achievement of this administration. When everything else . . . is forgotten . . . the steps we have taken toward the modernization of our constitution will still be remembered."[60] He could not have been more correct. The concrete groundwork had been put in place for use over the next several years.

A week later Governor Walter E. Edge stated in his inaugural that "by a decisive majority, which amazed every political prophet in the State, the voters have authorized, nay, demanded, that this Legislature revise the present Constitution. . . . There is no greater responsibility in American government than this mandate the people of our State have placed on us."[61] He went on to make a plea for a state constitution as fundamental law only, without special interest or other "short-lived" matters, which would include most of the improvements suggested by Edison and included in the Hendrickson draft.

At the beginning of 1944 an attempt had been made to obtain a court order invalidating the referendum authorizing the legislature to draft a constitution on the ground that such a mechanism was not authorized in the 1844 Constitution. The Supreme Court, accepting the argument presented by Arthur T. Vanderbilt in defense of the referendum, ruled that the challenge presented a premature political question that the courts would not entertain (In re Borg).

Governor Edge referred to this case in his inaugural:

I submit to you . . . that the entire constitutional revision procedure, which has been in progress during the past two years, has been in the highest traditions of American constitutional theory and practice. It has been sustained by a bona fide constituent act of the people of New Jersey; and there is no review, judicial or otherwise, from a popular expression at once so definite and so clear in a field which has been, and remains, exclusively a matter of popular action at the polls.

Edge predicted the development of a "document adequate to the occasions of the next hundred years" and indicated that this was the "opportunity of a century."[62]

A joint legislative committee, working from the 1942 Hendrickson draft and after very brief public hearings, quickly presented a very similar version to the legislature. The "Edge Draft," as it came to be known, was approved by the legislature but defeated soundly at the polls in November 1944 amid heated partisan and other political controversy.[63] Thus, in the early 1940s, both the constitutional commission and legislative routes to constitutional revision had failed.

Governor Edge expressed extreme disappointment in his 1945 Message to the Legislature but vowed to accomplish needed reforms even without constitutional revision. He made great strides in terms of administrative restructuring and fiscal and civil service reform.[64] The idea of a bipartisan, elected constitutional convention, limited in certain aspects (equal county representation in the Senate) by an authorizing vote of the people, came under serious consideration in 1945, laying the groundwork for the 1947 Constitutional Convention. Nineteen forty-five saw a number of half-hearted attempts at piecemeal state constitutional amendments, but they did not receive legislative approval. The 1946 session approved several proposed amendments, but their consideration in the 1947 session was overshadowed by the culmination of seven years of attempts at revision during that year.

With the war at an end Alfred E. Driscoll campaigned for governor on a platform of an open constitutional convention that would not have authority to change the method of representation in the legislature. After being elected and riding a momentum similar to his predecessors, but having the benefit of their experience, he stated in his inaugural that the move for constitutional revision dated back to Governor Joel Parker's call for a convention in 1873. He described the recent apparent paradox of the people voting to permit the legislature to draft a constitution but rejecting its product. Driscoll, accurately it seems, attributed this not to respect for the 1844 Constitution, but rather to the partisan atmosphere surrounding the development and presentation of the Edge Draft. He characterized the 1844 document as "hopelessly out of step with the requirements of our modern industrialized age. It handicaps rather than helps our efforts to achieve good government and sound fiscal policies." He reassured the small counties, however, that their interests would be protected in a constitutional convention— not by a limitation emanating from the legislature—but by the expressed will of the people themselves.[65]

Virtually all of the interests that had participated on either side of the issue of constitutional revision since 1940 fell in line behind Driscoll's proposal. Within a month the legislature had passed a constitutional convention bill under which the voters would, at the June 1947 election, both vote on the question of whether there should be a convention, instructed to retain the method of legislative representation, and then for delegates.[66]

The people approved the question of a constitutional convention by better than a five-to-one margin. At the same time, in a remarkably bipartisan atmosphere, they elected delegates to the eighty-one person convention. The convention met in the summer of 1947 on the Rutgers campus in New Brunswick and produced what has been viewed as among the best of the state constitutions. Building on the work of 1942–44, around much of which a consensus had by now developed, the constitution established a strong governor who could succeed himself and was the only official elected on a statewide basis. The gubernatorial veto was strengthened, and the executive branch was simplified and brought directly under his control. The Bill of Rights was modernized to provide equal rights for women, an antidiscrimination provision, and collective bargaining rights for labor. The judiciary was streamlined, responding finally to a century of attempted reforms, under a chief justice, who served as administrative head of all the courts. The Supreme Court was given rulemaking power over legal practice and procedure and over the legal profession. The method of representation in the legislature was, of course, beyond the reach of the convention, but terms of legislators were extended to two and four years, and the budget process was simplified by the requirement of a single, annual appropriations bill. Most of the procedural restrictions dating from the 1870s were retained, and the main area of contention was over the legislature's authority in the area of gambling. Once having achieved constitutional status in 1897 and 1939, it was impossible to return it to mere legislative regulation. Finally, a compromise resulted in a provision that would require a public referendum on any new forms of gambling (horse racing had already been approved in the 1939 referendum on that amendment). In the area of taxation policy, a new taxation and finance article was created, and the mandate of "true value" assessment of property for taxation was eliminated, to be replaced by the requirement that all property within a taxing unit be assessed according to a uniform standard.

The amendment process was modified to permit the legislature to submit an amendment to the people at the next general election if it received a three-fifths vote in each house. If the amendment received less than a three-fifths, but more than a majority vote, it had to be approved the next year before being submitted to the voters. Rejected amendments could not be resubmitted to the voters for at least three years.

The 1947 Constitution was ratified overwhelmingly by the voters and took effect in 1948. It represented the culmination of decades of attempted constitutional reform, but was particularly influenced by the 1942 and 1944 constitutional drafts and by Governor Edge's administrative and fiscal reforms of 1944–45. In other words, it included many provisions ''whose time had come,'' or, in the words of Willard Hurst, ''such specific enactments of policy did not direct, but merely recorded, the currents of social change.''[67] The difficulty in achieving constitutional revision had permitted a consensus to build around the major reforms that were finally adopted.

CONSTITUTIONAL DEVELOPMENT FROM 1947

After the new constitution went into effect, there were, of course, a number of controversies to be decided. For example, in 1950 the Supreme Court decided that its rulemaking power was exclusive, thereby displacing any legislation on practice and procedure in the courts (Winberry v. Salisbury).[68] A legislative proposal to amend the constitution to overcome this case failed. Later in the 1950s the Court interpreted the new property tax provisions to provide major new avenues for reform in property tax assessment practices (Switz v. Township of Middleton). In 1953 the gambling provision was once again amended to permit certain bingo and raffles by charitable organizations.

Finally, in 1964, after nearly two centuries of operation, the system of equal representation for counties in the senate was struck down by the New Jersey Supreme Court in compliance with the U.S. Supreme Court's one-person-one-vote decisions (Jackman v. Bodine). The Court concluded that the legislature could call a constitutional convention without a vote of the people because a new apportionment system was mandated by the federal Constitution. A constitutional convention, limited to the matter of reapportioning the legislature, was called, and its recommendations were accepted by the voters.[69]

In 1974 the voters turned down a proposed state equal rights amendment for women, but these rights were already guaranteed by the 1947 Constitution.[70] Also in 1974 the voters turned down an amendment that would have permitted state-sponsored casino gambling. In 1976, however, a reformulated casino gambling amendment limited to Atlantic City, which mandated strict state regulation and directed tax revenues toward the elderly and disabled, attracted the necessary voter support for adoption.

CONCLUSION

One might almost say that the romance, the poetry, and even the drama of American politics are deeply embedded in the many state constitutions promulgated since the publication of Paine's Common Sense, the Declaration of Independence, and the Virginia Bill of Rights.[71]

The development of constitutionalism in New Jersey has spanned the spectrum: from an almost unnoticed 1776 Constitution, which soon became the subject of major criticism; to an 1844 Constitution, which was also relatively unremarkable, but which governed for over a century; to a 1947 Constitution that was recognized immediately as a model of a brief, streamlined state governing document. In the words of legal historian Lawrence Friedman, New Jersey's 1947 Constitution presents a "paradigm case" of a "technician's constitution."[72] New Jersey's governor is recognized as among the strongest leaders of a well-organized executive. The state Supreme Court is known as among the top state courts in the country. This is a strange pattern—almost two centuries of state constitutional obscurity, followed by forty years of leadership.

New Jersey's pattern of state constitutional development has been significantly different from that experienced by other states. As one of the original thirteen states, its first constitution predated the federal Constitution by more than a decade. That first constitution drew little positive comment, either from contemporaries or from later observers. Since then, New Jersey has utilized relatively few constitutions—three if one does not count the major revisions accomplished through the amendment process in 1875—in its more than two centuries of statehood. Furthermore, each of these constitutions was relatively brief compared to those of other states. Therefore, the brevity of the 1947 Constitution should not be a great surprise.

Thus New Jersey has not seen fit to follow Thomas Jefferson's advice that a state constitution be regularly revised, "so that it may be handed on, with periodical repairs, from generation to generation."[73] New Jersey's state constitutional text has not been "repaired" very often. This is not to say, however, that the topic of state constitutional change has not been a prominent matter of political and legal discussion throughout New Jersey's history. As we have seen, the topic of state constitutional change was almost a constant topic of political and legal discussion. This dialogue simply did not lead to actual constitutional change very often. New Jersey's experience, therefore, may be seen as contrary to a recent conclusion about other state constitutions:

We should not overemphasize the importance of constitutional change by interpretation at the state level, however. Because of the detailed language of most state constitutions, conservative legislatures and judges have been inclined to follow a rather strict construction. There has been far less interpretative constitutional development at the state than at the national level. As a method of constitutional change, it is probably true that interpretation has been less important than the more formal processes of amendment and revision.[74]

As a result of the relative stability of New Jersey's state constitutional texts, change in the operation of the constitutional system and changes in it have been accomplished first by extraconstitutional arrangements and by judicial interpretation of the constitution. These two methods of change become more important in the absence of frequent revision or amendment of the constitutional text. Furthermore, New Jersey seems to have been able simply to "make do" with its defective constitutional provisions. Finally, as in any state, many aspects of state governmental operation occur outside of the formal constitutional structure.

Several things seem apparent from New Jersey's relative reluctance to initiate constitutional change. Much of the resistance to even discussing any state constitutional change had to do with a single issue written into the 1776 Constitution: equal representation for counties in the upper house. This not only inhibited state constitutional change itself, but contributed to the continuation of a relatively difficult amendment mechanism in the 1844 Constitution. This continued to frustrate constitutional change until even after 1947.

In the absence of a relatively easy road to state constitutional amendment, New Jersey was spared the waves of "constitutional legislation" on matters which, although theoretically better left to legislative discretion, are inserted into the constitutional text by the powerful interest groups of the day. Such interest groups utilize the state constitution as a lawmaking tool sometimes to bypass an unresponsive legislature, but always to achieve more permanence than they can obtain with regular statutes. Such constitutional legislation, in turn, often spawns more constitutional text as consensus on the matter changes and exceptions to the constitutional provision seems necessary. So, even though New Jersey seemed unable to respond adequately to its perceived constitutional deficiencies, this same inability operated to spare New Jersey the glut of amendments that have bloated other states' constitutions. The gambling provision seems to be the only exception, although it is probably an understandable one.

The structural and political obstacles to state constitutional change have meant that a very strong consensus was necessary before change could occur. By the same token, once some facilitating event or political compromise made constitutional change possible, the consensus was already there for the substance of the changes. This is what happened in 1844, 1875, and 1947.

In each of these three instances of New Jersey constitutional change, the facilitator of change was the governor. Although under the constitutions prior to 1947 the governor was "weak," in each instance he was able to devise a political formula that made state constitutional change seem almost effortless. Upon closer examination, it is clear that each of these governors built on prior suggested changes and analyzed the political reasons for failure of the suggested changes. In this way, each was able to break the log jam of state constitutional rigidity to accomplish needed reforms.

The 1947 Constitution, together with the elimination of equal senate representation for counties in 1965 under the mandate of the U.S. Supreme Court, has released New Jersey from state constitutional rigidity. By 1947, however, a state constitutional culture seems to have developed in New Jersey—a culture in which change in the state constitutional text is not made lightly, and this has persisted to the present day.

Ultimately, the test of a state constitution is how it functions. In the words of Frank Grad: "The least we may demand of our state constitutions is that they interpose no obstacle to the necessary exercise of state powers in response to state residents' real needs and active demands for service."[75] New Jersey's constitution now clearly meets this minimum test and provides much more.

NOTES

1. Elisha P. Douglass, *Rebels and Democrats: The Struggle for Equal Political Rights and Majority Rule During the American Revolution* (Chapel Hill: University of North Carolina Press, 1955), 66.

2. Julian P. Boyd, *Fundamental Laws and Constitutions of New Jersey, 1664–1964* (Princeton: D. Van Nostrand Co., 1964), 24. See also Charles Erdman, Jr., *The New Jersey Constitution of 1776* (Princeton: Princeton University Press, 1929), 34–37. This conclusion has recently been challenged on the basis of comparisons of the final draft with an earlier version, and because New Jersey's extreme legislative dominance did not seem to square with John Adams' ideas of "balanced government," which had apparently been so influential on Sergeant. On these grounds, John P. Furman has recently concluded that the drafter of at least the early version of the constitution was John Cooper of Woodbury. John P. Furman, "The Drafting of the New Jersey Constitution of 1776," (unpublished manuscript). The answer to this puzzle may never be known with certainty.

3. Sergeant to Samuel Adams, Bristol, Pa., June 24, 1776, quoted in Ruth Bogin, *Abraham Clark and the Quest for Equality in the Revolutionary Era, 1774–1794* (Rutherford, N.J.: Fairleigh Dickinson University Press, 1982), 40.

4. Cecelia Kenyon, "Constitutionalism in Revolutionary America," in *Nomos XX: Constitutionalism*, Roland J. Pennock and John W. Chapman, eds. (New York: New York University Press, 1979), 91–92. It is possible that this could account for the sharp reduction in the number of delegates voting for the constitution. See John E. O'Connor, *William Patterson: Lawyer and Statesman, 1745–1806* (New Brunswick, N.J.: Rutgers University Press, 1979), 85.

5. Larry R. Gerlach, ed., *New Jersey in the American Revolution 1763–1783: A Documentary History* (Trenton: New Jersey Historical Commission, 1975), 216. References to the 1776 New Jersey Constitution are to this source.

6. Chief Justice Fredrick Smyth to the Middlesex Grand Jury, April 1776, in Gerlach, *New Jersey in the American Revolution*, 187.

7. Charles Erdman, Jr., *The New Jersey Constitution*, 43–69. See also M.J.C. Vile, *Constitutionalism and the Separation of Powers* (New York: Oxford University Press, Clarendon, 1967), 133. ("The Constitution of New Jersey was little more than a copy of a colonial charter, although it remained in force until 1844.")

8. Erdman, *The New Jersey Constitution*, 69.

9. For an important study of the early state bills of rights, diminishing the differences between those states with and without such declarations, see William E. Nelson and Robert C. Palmer, *Liberty and Community: Constitution and Rights in the Early American Republic* (New York: Oceana, 1987).

10. This fascinating example of New Jersey's early, expansive voting rights is traced

thoroughly in Mary Philbrook, "Woman's Suffrage in New Jersey Prior to 1807," *Proceedings of N.J. Hist. Soc.* 57 (1939): 87; J. R. Pole, "The Suffrage in New Jersey, 1790–1807," *Proceedings of the N.J. Hist. Soc.* 71 (1953):39; Marion Thompson Wright, "Negro Suffrage in New Jersey, 1776–1875," *Journal of Negro History* 33 (1948): 168; Erdman, *The New Jersey Constitution*, 82–87.

11. Larry R. Gerlach, "Power to the People: Popular Sovereignty, Republicanism, and the Legislature in Revolutionary New Jersey," in *The Development of the New Jersey Legislature From Colonial Times to the Present*, William C. Wright, ed. (Trenton: New Jersey Historical Commission, 1979), 21.

12. Jackson Turner Main, *Political Parties Before the Constitution* (Chapel Hill: University of North Carolina Press, 1973), 169. For an excellent treatment of taxation issues in the New Jersey legislature, see Robert A. Becker, *Revolution, Reform, and the Politics of American Taxation, 1763–1783* (Baton Rouge: Louisiana State University Press, 1980), 166–73.

13. Walter F. Dodd, *The Revision and Amendment of State Constitutions*, (New York: DeCapo reprint, 1970), 32; *Wilson's Acts of the General Assembly of the State of New Jersey, 1777*, 24.

14. Donald S. Lutz, *Popular Consent and Popular Control: Whig Political Theory in the Early State Constitutions* (Baton Rouge: Louisiana State University Press, 1980), 62. See also ibid., 66, 81.

15. This case is not available in the law reports, but is discussed in Austin Scott, "*Holmes v. Walton*: The New Jersey Precedent," *American Historical Review* 4 (1898–99): 456; and Erdman, *The New Jersey Constitution*, 90–92.

16. Edward S. Corwin, "The Progress of Constitutional Theory between the Declaration of Independence and the Meeting of the Philadelphia Convention," *American Historical Review* 30 (1925): 521. See also Edward S. Corwin, "The Establishment of Judicial Review," *Michigan Law Review* 9 (1910): 110–12.

17. Erdman, *The New Jersey Constitution*, 109. See also Bernard Siegan, *Economic Rights and the Constitution* (Chicago: University of Chicago Press, 1980), 27–40. Erdman describes an interesting 1795 case, Taylor v. Reading, which invalidated a statute authorizing paper money rather than specie payments on ex post facto grounds. Erdman speculated that the case was based on the federal Constitution's ex post facto clause, but applying the prohibition to a *civil* case, he pointed out, was a much broader reading than the United States Supreme Court's 1798 Calder v. Bull opinion limiting the ex post facto clause to *criminal* cases. Erdman, *The New Jersey Constitution*, 92, n. 18.

18. John Bebout, "Striking a Balance: Demand for an Independent Judiciary, 1776–1844," in *Jersey Justice: Three Hundred Years of the New Jersey Judiciary*, Carla Vivian Bello and Arthur T. Vanderbilt II, eds. (Newark, N.J.: Institute for Continuing Legal Education, 1978), 117, 124, 131.

19. I am indebted to Herbert Ershkowitz for this interesting insight. See generally Herbert Ershkowitz, *The Origins of the Whig and Democratic Parties: New Jersey Politics, 1820–1837* (Washington, D.C.: University Press of America, 1982).

20. Duane Lockard, *The New Jersey Governor: A Study in Political Power* (Princeton: Van Nostrand Co., 1964), 40–41; Richard P. McCormick, "The First Election of Governor William Livingston,: *Proceedings of the N.J. Hist. Soc.* 65 (April 1974): 92. "The architects of the constitution envisioned a political order marked by strong legislative and weak executive authority, but the exigencies of the years 1776–83 produced the opposite."

Gerlach, "Power to the People," 35. See generally Jackson Turner Main, *The Sovereign States: 1775–1783* (New York: Franklin Watts, 1973), 190.

21. *New York Spectator*, April 13, 1799, quoted in Frederick M. Herrmann, "The Constitution of 1844 and Political Change in Antebellum New Jersey," *New Jersey History* 101 (Spring/Summer 1983): 30–31; John Bebout, "Introduction," *Proceedings of the New Jersey State Constitutional Convention of 1844* (1942), liii.

22. Bebout, "Striking a Balance," p. 122.

23. State v. Parkhurst, 9 N.J.L. 427, 442–43 (1828). This was an 1802 decision, but it was not reported until 1828.

24. Erdman, *New Jersey Constitution*, 117.

25. Bebout, "Introduction," lxix. Bebout attributes this point to Woodrow Wilson.

26. Erdman, *New Jersey Constitution*, 116, 130–35.

27. Herrmann, "The Constitution of 1844," 29.

28. Erdman, *New Jersey Constitution*, 137.

29. See Bott v. Sec. of State, 62 N.J.L. 107, 121, 40 A. 740, 745, (Sup. Ct. 1898), aff'd 63 N.J.L. 289, 43 A. 744 (E. & A. 1899).

30. Daniel Elazar, "The Principles and Traditions Underlying State Constitutions, "*Publius: The Journal of Federalism* 12 (1982): 15.

31. Robert J. Steinfeld, "Property and Suffrage in the Early American Republic," *Stanford Law Review* 41 (1989): 335.

32. N.J. Constitution Art. III (1776). See Jackman v. Bodine, 43 N.J. 453, 459, 463, 205 A.2d 713, 716, 718 (1964).

33. Bebout and Harrison, "The Working of the New Jersey Constitution," 339.

34. For an in-depth discussion of these debates see John O. Bigelow, "New Jersey Constitutional Convention of 1844: Debate on Future Amendments," *Proceedings of the New Jersey Historical Society* 59 (July 1941): 183.

35. Bebout, "Introduction," xcviii; Paul v. Gloucester Co., 50 N.J.L. 585, 591 (E & A 1888).

36. Herrmann, "The Constitution of 1844," 43–44. At least two of these bills were passed over the governor's veto. Ibid., 44 n.67.

37. Arthur Zilversmit, *The First Emancipation: The Abolition of Slavery in the North* (Chicago: University of Chicago Press, 1967), 193, 218–20.

38. State v. Post, 20 N.J.L. 368, 375, 380 (1845). Chief Justice Joseph C. Hornblower, a delegate to the convention a year earlier, dissented without opinion.

39. Herrmann, "The Constitution of 1844," 39. See also Bebout and Harrison, "The Working of the New Jersey Constitution," 339.

40. Bennett M. Rich, *The Government and Administration of New Jersey* (New York: Thomas Crowell Co., 1957), 18.

41 Ibid.; Bebout, "Introduction," cv–cvi. Governor Parker's address is in the *Journal of New Jersey Senate*, 1873, 21. His recommendations on constitutional reform begin at page 48. The quote is at page 49.

42. *Journal of New Jersey Senate*, 1873, 1068; *Minutes of the New Jersey General Assembly*, 1873, 1426, 1431.

43. "Proclamation by the Governor," April 16, 1873, *1873 Laws of New Jersey*, 843–44.

44. *Journal of New Jersey Senate*, 1874, 43.

45. Bebout, "Introduction," cvi.

46. *Journal of New Jersey Senate*, 1882, 71.

47. Mary Philbrook's career, including this litigation, is examined in Barbara Burns Petrick, "Mary Philbrook, Lawyer and Feminist: Opening the Practice of Law to Women and Establishing a Constitutional Basis for Sex Equality in New Jersey," *Women's Rights Law Reporter* 4 (Summer 1978): 253; Barbara Petrick, "Right or Privilege? The Admission of Mary Philbrook to the Bar," *New Jersey History* 97 (Summer 1979): 91.

48. Mina C. Van Winkle, "New Jersey First," *Women Lawyers Journal* 5 (October 1915): 1.

49. This problem is discussed generally in Kenneth C. Sears and Charles V. Laughlin, "A Study in Constitutional Rigidity," *University of Chicago Law Review* 11 (1944):374.

50. *New Jersey Legislative Manual* (1913), 664.

51. See John E. Bebout and Julius Kass, "The Status of Constitutional Conventions in New Jersey," *University of Newark Law Review* 3 (1938):146; John Bebout and Julius Kass, "How Can New Jersey Get a New Constitution?" *University of Newark Law Review* 6 (1941): 1.

52. Richard J. Connors, *The Process of Constitutional Revision in New Jersey, 1940— 1947* (New York: National Municipal League, 1970), 14–15.

53. *1941 New Jersey Legislative Manual*, 664.

54. Connors, *The Process of Constitutional Revision*, 38–39.

55. Ibid., 41.

56. State of New Jersey, *Record of Proceedings before the Joint Committee Constituted Under Senate Concurrent Resolution No. 19* (1942). This contains the Report and Draft Constitution of the Hendrickson Commission.

57. State of New Jersey, *Record of Proceedings*, 549–51.

58. Ibid., 869.

59. Connors, *The Process of Constitutional Revision*, 68, 75.

60. *1944 Legislative Manual*, 657.

61. *1944 Legislative Manual*, 672.

62. Ibid., 676.

63. The proposed constitution of 1944 is found in *Laws of New Jersey*, 1944, 195–241 (Chapter 92).

64. Connors, *The Process of Constitutional Revision*, 116.

65. *1947 Legislative Manual*, 705–7.

66. *Laws of New Jersey*, 1947, 24–39 (Chapter 8).

67. James W. Hurst, *The Growth of American Law: The Law Makers* (Boston: Little, Brown & Co., 1950), 246.

68. This decision received national attention. See Benjamin Kaplan and Warren J. Greene, "The Legislature's Relationship to Judicial Rule Making: An Appraisal of Winberry v. Salisbury," *Harvard Law Review* 65 (1951):234, and Roscoe Pound, "Procedure Under Rules of Court in New Jersey," *Harvard Law Review* 66 (1952):28.

69. "Rediscovering the New Jersey E.R.A.: The Key to Successful Sex Discrimination Litigation," *Rutgers Law Journal* 17 (1986):273 n. 124.

70. See generally Arthur J. Sills and Alan B. Handler, "The Imbroglio of Constitutional Revision—Another By-Product of Reapportionment," *Rutgers Law Review* 20 (1965):1.

71. Dealey, *Growth of American State Constitutions*, p. 11.

72. Lawrence M. Friedman, "State Constitutions in Historical Perspective," *Annals* 496 (1988):39.

73. Jefferson to Samuel Kercheval, July 12, 1816, quoted in A. E. Dick Howard,

''Constitutional Revision: Virginia and the Nation,'' *University of Richmond Law Review* 9 (1974):1.

74. Elmer E. Cornwell, Jr., Jay S. Goodman, and Wayne R. Swanson, *State Constitutional Conventions: The Politics of the Revision Process In Seven States* (New York: Praeger Publishers, 1975), 8; Connors, *The Process of Constitutional Revision*, 9.

75. Frank P. Grad, ''The State Constitution: Its Function and Form in Our Time,'' *Virginia Law Review* 54 (1968):939.

Part II

New Jersey Constitution and Commentary

Part II provides a section-by-section analysis of the current New Jersey Constitution. It briefly delineates the origins of each provision and analyzes the major interpretations by the courts and, where relevant, the Attorney General.[1] Further, important discussions of the provision in the legal literature are referenced. In an attempt to avoid lengthy case references, more recent cases are cited where they rely on important, older cases. There is no attempt to trace earlier, important cases, where the text of the provision has been altered so as to relegate those earlier issues to only historical interest. The most important of such decisions, however, such as those leading directly to a change in the constitutional text, are treated in Part I, New Jersey Constitutional Development. The citations to cases discussed can be found in the Appendix (Table of Cases).

These section-by-section discussions should not be considered as necessarily exhaustive or as remaining up-to-date after the publication of this book. They cover the major interpretive issues arising under each provision, without covering every issue that may have arisen or that may arise in the future. These discussions should not be relied upon as legal advice nor as a substitute for specific legal research on an issue in which a reader may be interested.

PREAMBLE

> We, the people of the State of New Jersey, grateful to Almighty God for the civil and religious liberty which He hath so long permitted us to enjoy, and looking to Him for a blessing upon our endeavors to secure and transmit the same unimpaired to succeeding generations, do ordain and establish this Constitution.

This preamble is identical to that preceding the 1844 Constitution. The preamble is not actually a part of the constitution itself. As one New Jersey court said in 1910: "It is impossible to so construe the preamble as to write something into the constitution that its framers did not write into it" (Booth v. McGuinness). Still, the preamble makes it readily apparent that the source of authority for New Jersey's government is and continues to be the people of the state.

Article I

Rights and Privileges

Although the 1776 Constitution did not contain a Declaration of Rights, it provided in Article XXII that the common law of England "shall still remain in force," which many believed carried forward most of the "Rights of Englishmen" into New Jersey law. A separate article containing a Declaration of Rights appeared for the first time in New Jersey in 1844.

The 1947 version of the Bill of Rights was described by Governor Alfred E. Driscoll soon after its adoption as expressing "the social, political and economic ideals of the present day in a broader way than ever before in American constitutional history."[2] The New Jersey courts have, on a number of occasions since the early 1970s, interpreted the state Bill of Rights more broadly in order to provide more rights to citizens than are provided under the federal Constitution as interpreted by the U.S. Supreme Court.[3]

In civil liberties matters where there are both federal and state constitutional guarantees that are relevant to analyzing the issue, but the litigant claims more extensive protection under the state provision, the Supreme Court of New Jersey has taken several points of view. First, where there is no definitive U.S. Supreme Court precedent, the New Jersey Supreme Court will rule on the federal interpretation issue in a "predictive" way (State v. Hartley). Second, where there is a clear U.S. Supreme Court precedent on the federal issue, the New Jersey Supreme Court seems to have adopted the "factor," or "criteria" approach. Under this approach, the U.S. Supreme Court's interpretation of the analogous federal constitutional provision is the starting point for analysis. The Supreme Court's interpretation will be adopted as the interpretation of the related New Jersey constitutional provision unless there is some identifiable factor that would justify the Court's interpretation of the state provision to provide broader protections than those available under the federal provision. This technique first appeared in Justice Alan Handler's concurring opinion in State v. Hunt in 1982 and was endorsed by the full Court the next year in State v. Williams. Justice Handler listed seven criteria or standards that would justify a result different from the Supreme Court's: (1) textual differences in the constitutions; (2) "legislative history" of the provision indicating a broader meaning than the federal provision; (3) state law predating the Supreme Court decision; (4) differences in federal and state structure; (5) subject matter of particular state or local interest; (6) particular state history or traditions; and (7) public attitudes in the state. He concluded that reliance on such criteria demonstrates that a divergent state constitutional interpretation "does not spring from pure intuition but, rather, from a process that is reasonable and reasoned."

Justice Handler denied that his analysis created a presumption in favor of the U.S. Supreme Court result, but Justice Morris Pashman, in a separate concurrence, disagreed.[4] Importantly, Justice Pashman observed that such a presumption limits a state court's authority to interpret its own constitution.

The New Jersey Supreme Court thus appears to require some objectively verifiable difference between state and federal constitutional analysis—whether textual, decisional, or historical—to justify a state court embracing a different interpretation. This view implies that in the absence of one or more of the criteria identified, it is illegitimate for a state court to reject the reasoning or result of a U.S. Supreme Court decision.

It is certainly possible to criticize the use of the criteria or factor approach,[5] and, in fact, the Supreme Court of New Jersey does not always adhere to its announced approach.[6] There are a number of alternative ways for state courts to address state constitutional protections that are analogous to federal constitutional protections.[7] Nevertheless, the New Jersey courts' endorsement of the factor or criteria approach suggests an important and useful set of techniques for addressing state constitutional civil liberties claims in areas where there are analogous federal rights.

Several justices of the Supreme Court of New Jersey have written law review articles about their views on interpreting state constitutional rights provisions.[8]

The Supreme Court of New Jersey has held, as a general matter, the rights guaranteed in the state constitution are enforceable in court even in the absence of implementing legislation or a *statutorily* created cause of action, that is, a law passed by the legislature specifically authorizing court suits to enforce constitutional provisions.[9] In the words of Chief Justice Richard Hughes in King v. South Jersey National Bank, "Just as the Legislature cannot abridge constitutional rights by its enactments, it cannot curtail them through its silence, and the judicial obligation to protect the fundamental rights of individuals is as old as this country."

NATURAL AND UNALIENABLE RIGHTS

1. All persons are by nature free and independent, and have certain natural and unalienable rights, among which are those of enjoying and defending

life and liberty, of acquiring, possessing, and protecting property, and of
pursuing and obtaining safety and happiness.

This broad provision, similar to the initial provisions contained in Virginia's
famous 1776 Declaration of Rights and the 1780 Massachusetts Declaration of
Rights, forms the textual basis for the rights of due process of law, equal
protection of the law, privacy, the "right to die," vested rights in property, and
several other important New Jersey constitutional doctrines. Many of these rights
are protected under more specific provisions of the federal Constitution. An
extremely important revision of the original 1844 language was adopted at the
1947 constitutional convention: the words "all *persons*" were substituted for
"all *men*" in an explicit move to secure equal rights for women.[10]

Equal Protection

Among the most important, but also most difficult to apply, constitutional
rights are those requiring equal protection under the law. These are, generally
speaking, aimed at keeping the government from singling out certain groups for
either better or worse treatment than others without good reason.

The New Jersey Constitution, like most state constitutions, does not contain
an equal protection clause like that found in the Fourteenth Amendment to the
federal Constitution.[11] New Jersey courts have, however, held that Article I,
paragraph 1 implicitly includes a "concept of equal protection" (McKenney v.
Byrne; Washington Nat'l Ins. Co. v. Bd. of Review). The courts have often
equated the state doctrine with the equal protection clause of the Fourteenth
Amendment to the federal Constitution (McKenney v. Byrne), but it is clear
that New Jersey's equal protection doctrine is not "coterminous" with federal
doctrine (Planned Parenthood of N.Y.C. v. State) and may, in fact, provide
broader protections for persons in New Jersey than provided under federal equal
protection doctrine (Peper v. Princeton University Board of Trustees). Recently,
however, the courts have tended to follow federal equal protection analysis
(Barone v. Dept. of Human Services; Sykes v. Propane Power Corp).

Federal equal protection analysis, as articulated by the U.S. Supreme Court,
has evolved into a relatively limited view of enforcement based on the nature
of the classification, that is, race, sex, and so forth, or the importance of the
right involved, that is, voting, marriage, and so forth. Equal protection in New
Jersey is frequently analyzed under a more flexible approach than at the federal
level, allowing the court to apply a balancing test in appropriate cases. Chief
Justice Joseph Weintraub enunciated this test in Robinson v. Cahill (1973):

[W]e have not found helpful the concept of a "fundamental" right. No one has successfully defined the term for this purpose . . . if a right is somehow found to be "fundamental," there remains the question as to what State interest is "compelling" and
there, too, we find little, if any, light. Mechanical approaches to the delicate problem of

judicial intervention under either the equal protection or the due process clauses may only divert the court from the meritorious issue or delay consideration of it. Ultimately, a court must weigh the nature of the restraint or the denial against the apparent public justification, and decide whether the State action is arbitrary.

Under this approach, a right need not be labelled "fundamental" to trigger searching judicial review, which will balance the need for the legislative or executive action against the infringement of the right at issue (see also Abbott v. Burke; Greenberg v. Kimmelman).

The New Jersey Supreme Court has also recognized that a standard or statute that is not specifically based on a discrimination-generating classification or right may nevertheless be discriminatory because of the means employed to achieve the objective. This component of New Jersey equal protection was established by the "means-focused" test developed in Borough of Collingswood v. Ringgold. This test emphasizes the fitness of the means chosen to further a valid purpose. The Court in Ringgold found the means employed in a local ordinance (the disparate registration of solicitors) reasonable and, thus, not violative of equal protection. The Court ruled that Collingswood's interests in not unduly burdening local community solicitation efforts (church, civic, and charity groups in particular) justified the differing requirements of the ordinance.

New Jersey courts may, therefore, use either a balancing test or a means-focused approach. A leading example is Right to Choose v. Byrne.[12] In this 1982 decision the New Jersey Supreme Court rejected the U.S. Supreme Court's 1980 decision in Harris v. McRae and held that terminating medical assistance funding for abortions that were necessary to protect the health of the mother violated Article I, paragraph 1, of the New Jersey Constitution. The New Jersey Court concluded that "in balancing the protection of a woman's health and her fundamental right to privacy against the asserted state interest in protecting potential life, we conclude that the governmental interference is unreasonable."

There are several other provisions in the New Jersey Constitution that reflect equality concerns, such as Article I, paragraph 5, and Article IV, Section VII, paragraphs 7, 8, and 9, and sometimes the New Jersey courts refer to them together (Planned Parenthood of N.Y.C. v. State). However, each has its distinctive history, text, and specific judicial interpretation and therefore warrants separate analysis.[13]

Privacy

The contours of New Jersey's right to privacy, implicit in Article I, paragraph 1, were neatly captured by Justice Sidney Schreiber in State v. Saunders:

We have hitherto recognized that this provision encompasses an individual right of privacy. *In re Quinlan*, 70 N.J. 10, 40 *cert. den sub nom. Garger* v. *New Jersey*, 429 U.S. 922, 97 S. Ct. 319, 50 L. Ed.2d 289 (1976). Article I, par. 1 is almost a copy of the comparable provision in the 1844 Constitution. In a monograph prepared for the 1947 New Jersey Constitutional Convention, Dean Heckel stated that "among the rights included" in Article 1, par. 1 of the 1844 Constitution is a "right of privacy." Heckel, "The Bill of Rights," in II *Constitutional Convention of 1947*, 1336 at 1339. He relied upon *McGovern v. Van Riper*, 137 N.J. Eq. 24, 33 (Ch. 1945), in which the court wrote that the right of privacy "is one of the 'natural and inalienable rights' recognized in article 1, section 1 of the constitution of this state." No language change made in Article I, par. 1 by the 1947 Constitutional Convention would affect this construction.

The Saunders decision found certain adult sexual activities to be protected by the right to privacy. Also within this broad right are matters such as the "right to die" (In re Quinlan; In re Jobes) and rights of unrelated persons to live in one household despite zoning restrictions to the contrary (State v. Baker; Borough of Glassboro v. Vallorosi).

Due Process of Law

The right to due process of law is also implied in Article I, paragraph 1 (Nicoletta v. North Jersey District Water Supply Commission). There are two separate components of the right to due process: (1) the requirement of certain *procedures* before one may be deprived of property or other important interests; and (2) protections of the *substance* of one's property or other important interests from governmental intrusion.

In the procedural context, New Jersey courts have required, for example, effective notice and hearing opportunities before tax foreclosure (Township of Montville v. Block 69, Lot 10) or loss of public employment (Cunningham v. Dept. of Civil Service). With respect to substantive due process, a good example of protection is in the area of the limitations on the retroactive application of statutes (Rothman v. Rothman) and where statutes are challenged as beyond the legislature's power to regulate for health, safety, and the general welfare (Matter of C.V.S. Pharmacy). Another way substantive due process is described is in terms of limits on the deprivation of "vested rights." The New Jersey Supreme Court has defined a vested right as "a present fixed interest which in right reason and natural justice should be protected against arbitrary state action—an innately just and imperative right that an enlightened free society, sensitive to inherent and irrefragable individual rights, cannot deny." (Pennsylvania Greyhound Lines, Inc. v. Rosenthal). Primarily, the notion of vested rights applies to property rights, but it can be applied to other personal rights such as those involving employment, family, and so forth. Finally, an important doctrine recognized by New Jersey courts that is very close to the requirement of due process of law is the doctrine of fundamental fairness. While this is not actually a *constitutional* doctrine, it is closely related to due process and deserves mention here.[14]

POLITICAL POWER; OBJECT OF GOVERNMENT

2. All political power is inherent in the people. Government is instituted for the protection, security, and benefit of the people, and they have the

right at all times to alter or reform the same, whenever the public good may require it.

This provision, together with the preamble, restates the underlying source of authority for the adoption of, and changes in, state constitutions. It includes the Jeffersonian principle that each generation has the right to decide on its form of government by "recurrence to fundamental principles." It has been held, however, not to apply to local governments so as to limit legislative restrictions on how often the electorate may vote on a change in the form of municipal government (Bucino v. Malone).

RIGHTS OF CONSCIENCE; RELIGIOUS FREEDOM

3. No person shall be deprived of the inestimable privilege of worshipping Almighty God in a manner agreeable to the dictates of his own conscience; nor under any pretense whatever be compelled to attend any place of worship contrary to his faith and judgement; nor shall any person be obliged to pay tithes, taxes, or other rates for building or repairing any church or churches, place or places of worship, or for the maintenance of any minister or ministry, contrary to what he believes to be right or has deliberately and voluntarily engaged to perform.

This paragraph is nearly verbatim from Article XVIII of the 1776 Constitution. It appeared as Article I, section 3, in the 1844 Constitution and was carried over in the 1947 Constitution. This provision, in typical fashion for state constitutions, guarantees religious freedom in much broader detail than the federal Constitution. It deals basically with the exercise of religious freedom and is usually read together with paragraph 4 prohibiting religious tests and preferences for particular religious sects, and paragraph 5 concerning religious discrimination. Despite the greater detail contained in paragraphs 3 and 4, the New Jersey Supreme Court has tended to equate them with the federal First Amendment religion guarantees (Schaad v. Ocean Grove Camp Meeting Ass'n.; Right to Choose v. Byrne. But see Marsa v. Wernik). The Court has held that an adult person's religious beliefs may not have to be honored in a life threatening situation calling for a blood transfusion (John F. Kennedy Memorial Hospital v. Heston).

The civil courts will usually refrain from interfering in the internal operations of religious institutions, particularly where interpretations of religious doctrine would be required. New Jersey courts, however, will adjudicate rights of, for example, membership under established procedures of a religious institution (Hardwick v. First Baptist Church).

ESTABLISHMENT OF RELIGIOUS SECT; RELIGIOUS OR RACIAL TEST FOR PUBLIC OFFICE

> 4. There shall be no establishment of one religious sect in preference to another; no religious or racial test shall be required as a qualification for any office or public trust.

This paragraph has its origin in Article XIX of the 1776 Constitution, which banned establishment of one religious sect in preference to another, but stated that only Protestants could serve in state government.

The provision in the 1844 Constitution contained what is now found in paragraph 5 prohibiting denial of civil rights on the basis of religious principles. In 1947 that clause was transferred to the new paragraph 5 and expanded to prohibit *racial* as well as religious discrimination.

The legislative delegation of municipal powers to a camp meeting association has been invalidated by the New Jersey Supreme Court (State v. Celmer). Furthermore, the Court has observed that this paragraph "is less pervasive, literally, than the Federal provision" (Resnick v. East Brunswick Board of Education; Marsa v. Wernik). For this reason, in establishment of religion cases, the New Jersey courts tend to focus on federal constitutional doctrine, except where an actual religious preference is at issue (Tudor v. Board of Education of Borough of Rutherford).

DENIAL OF RIGHTS; DISCRIMINATION; SEGREGATION

> 5. No person shall be denied the enjoyment of any civil or military right, nor be discriminated against in the exercise of any civil or military right, nor be segregated in the militia or in the public schools, because of religious principles, race, color, ancestry or national origin.

This provision had its origin in Article XIX of the 1776 Constitution, which stated that no *Protestant* could be denied the enjoyment of a civil right because of religious principles. Article I, section 4, of the 1844 Constitution provided that "no person shall be denied the enjoyment of any civil right merely on account of his religious principles." The 1947 convention created this new section and expanded it to include military as well as civil rights, discrimination in the exercise of rights in addition to strict denial of rights, and specific references to segregation. The convention broadened the whole section to include race, color, ancestry, or national origin beyond the earlier "religious principles."

The courts have looked to the paragraph as providing support for expansive civil rights legislation. The Supreme Court stated in Levitt and Sons, Inc. v. Division Against Discrimination:

In approaching the construction of the statute it is necessary to be mindful of the clear and positive policy of our State against discrimination as embodied in N.J. Constitution, Article I, paragraph 5. Effectuation of that mandate calls for liberal interpretation of any legislative enactment designed to implement it. .

Many of the sorts of discrimination and segregation proscribed in this paragraph are now regulated by statute. One case has interpreted this provision to apply to discrimination on the basis of sex (Gallagher v. City of Bayonne). The New Jersey Supreme Court has declined to decide whether this paragraph applies to discrimination on the basis of age (Shaner v. Horizon Bancorp.). Also, this provision has been referred to, together with paragraph 1, as providing for equal protection of the laws.

LIBERTY OF SPEECH AND OF THE PRESS; LIBEL; PROVINCE OF JURY

> 6. Every person may freely speak, write and publish his sentiments on all subjects, being responsible for the abuse of that right. No law shall be passed to restrain or abridge the liberty of speech or of the press. In all prosecutions or indictments for libel, the truth may be given in evidence to the jury; and if it shall appear to the jury that the matter charged as libelous is true, and was published with good motives and for justifiable ends, the party shall be acquitted; and the jury shall have the right to determine the law and the fact.

This paragraph was carried over verbatim from Article I, section 5, of the 1844 Constitution and must be considered together with paragraph 18, concerning the right to assemble and petition. Interestingly, the guarantee here is stated as an *affirmative* right of the people, not merely a limit on government action as is contained in the First Amendment to the federal Constitution: "Congress shall pass no law . . . " (State v. Schmid; State v. Hunt). The New Jersey Supreme Court has, therefore, recognized certain rights to free speech and expression on property such as a private university that, although privately owned, has been opened for public use (State v. Schmid). New Jersey courts have limited this principle in contexts such as union organizing (Bellemead Development Corp. v. Schneider) and abortion protesting (Planned Parenthood of Monmouth County v. Cannizzaro; State v. Brown). Generally speaking, however, free speech matters have been analyzed under federal constitutional principles.

The New Jersey Supreme Court has read this provision to require access to the press to virtually all criminal proceedings, including pretrial hearings (State v. Williams). The Court concluded that a criminal defendant's right to a fair trial should be protected in other ways than closing hearings to the press.

This paragraph also makes prosecutions for libel the subject of special constitutional protections in order to protect the right of free speech from both criminal prosecutions and civil actions for defamation (Coleman v. Newark Morning Ledger Co.; State v. Browne).

FREEDOM FROM UNREASONABLE SEARCHES AND SEIZURES; WARRANT

> 7. The right of the people to be secure in their persons, houses, papers, and effects, against unreasonable searches and seizures, shall not be violated; and no warrant shall issue except upon probable cause, supported by oath or affirmation, and particularly describing the place to be searched and the papers and things to be seized.

This paragraph was carried over verbatim from Article I, section 6, of the 1844 Constitution. Although it prohibits "unreasonable searches and seizures" in language identical to the Fourth Amendment to the federal Constitution, this provision has been interpreted many times to afford greater protection than the U.S. Supreme Court has when applying the Fourth Amendment (State v. Johnson [1975]; State v. Alston; State v. Novembrino).

The basic rule set out by this provision is that in the absence of some genuine emergency (State v. Valencia), a search of a person or property must be authorized by a search warrant. A person may, of course, consent to a search without a warrant, but this consent must be based on knowledge of the warrant requirement and a voluntary waiver of that requirement (State v. Johnson [1975]). Where a search warrant is issued by a judicial officer, it must be based on "probable cause," which must be assessed prior to the issuance of the warrant (State v. Novembrino). Furthermore, the search warrant must be specific both with respect to the space to be searched and the items to be searched for, and not simply "general" (State v. Reldan).

Where a search is improperly conducted either without a warrant or pursuant to a defective warrant, the remedy is for the court to exclude the illegally seized evidence (State v. Novembrino). These rules apply to a wide range of circumstances. For example, the New Jersey Supreme Court has held that telephone conversations and records thereof are protected from intrusion without a warrant (State v. Hunt), but that automobiles may be searched without a warrant if probable cause exists (State v. Esteves). Also, the Supreme Court has held that evidence validly seized by federal officers under less restrictive federal search and seizure doctrine, which could not be seized under the state constitution without a warrant, may nonetheless be admitted in state courts (State v. Mollica).

The Appellate Division has recently held that mandatory urine tests for drug abuse by police officers in a narcotics unit, without probable cause or individualized suspicion, violate this provision (Fraternal Order of Police v. City of Newark).

PRESENTMENT OR INDICTMENT OF GRAND JURY; NECESSITY; EXCEPTIONS

8. No person shall be held to answer for a criminal offense, unless on the presentment or indictment of a grand jury, except in cases of impeachment, or in cases now prosecuted without indictment, or arising in the army or navy or in the militia, when in actual service in time of war or public danger.

This paragraph first appeared as Article I, section 9, of the 1844 Constitution. The 1947 convention substituted "or in cases now prosecuted without indictment," for the original language: "or in cases cognizable by justices of the peace," to take into account the abolition of justices of the peace.

A grand jury is made up of laypersons who investigate and receive evidence on criminal violations. The grand jury may hand down an indictment or a formal, written charge against a person. The indictment serves to inform both the defendant and the court of the facts alleged to constitute a criminal offence so that the defendant may frame a defense and the court may evaluate the legal sufficiency of the alleged facts to constitute the offense charged (State v. Winne; State v. LeFurge). A grand jury may also issue a presentment, which is addressed to matters of public concern, or conditions which ought to be remedied, but which does not indict any person (In re Presentment by Camden County Grand Jury; In re Presentment by Essex County Grand Jury). If, however, a presentment indicates that an indictable offense has occurred, a court may refer the presentment back to the grand jury with instructions to hand down an indictment (In re Presentment by Essex County Grand Jury).

The key question in determining the application of this provision is which offenses are technically considered "criminal" and, therefore, require an indictment by a grand jury. The New Jersey Supreme Court has stated in State v. Senno:

In New Jersey, whether a person charged with an offence is entitled to the protections afforded by indictment depends on whether the offense with which the person is charged is criminal. . . . Although certainly *penal* in nature, infractions which fall "within the generic category of 'petty offences' " are not, strictly speaking, criminal in nature, and, because the direct and collateral consequences of conviction are more "limited," those so charged may be tried without indictment.

Although one function of an indictment is to notify a defendant of the charge, this does not prevent a defendant from being found guilty of a lesser offense that is considered to be intended by the grand jury to have been "included" within the more serious crime charged in the indictment (State v. Talley; State v. LeFurge).

Prosecutors and courts have a duty to see to it that grand jurors are unbiased

(State v. Murphy). Defendants may obtain access to grand jury records and challenge the sufficiency of an indictment on the basis of improper grand jury procedures (State v. Del Fino). A motion to dismiss an indictment will be granted, however, only where it is "palpably" insufficient (State v. Ciba-Geigy Corp.).

TRIAL BY JURY; JURY OF SIX PERSONS; VERDICT IN CIVIL CAUSES; TRIAL OF MENTAL INCOMPETENCY WITHOUT JURY

> 9. The right of trial by jury shall remain inviolate; but the Legislature may authorize the trial of civil causes by a jury of six persons. The Legislature may provide that in any civil cause a verdict may be rendered by not less than five-sixths of the jury. The Legislature may authorize the trial of the issue of mental incompetency without a jury.

The guarantee of trial by jury has its origin in Article XXII of the 1776 Constitution: "that the inestimable right of trial by jury shall remain confirmed as a part of the law of this Colony, without repeal, forever." The final mandate of the 1776 section could not be taken as literally true, because jury trial rights have been modified by subsequent amendments to the provision. This is evident in the 1844 provision, Article I, section 7: "The right of trial by jury shall remain inviolate; but the legislature may authorize the trial of civil suits, when the matter in dispute does not exceed fifty dollars, by a jury of six men." The 1947 convention changed the word "men" to "persons" and added the two additional authorizations to the legislature to provide for five-sixths decisions in civil actions and mental incompetency cases without juries.

This provision concerns jury trial rights in both criminal and civil cases. In criminal cases this paragraph must be analyzed together with the paragraph 10 guarantee of an "impartial jury." The right to jury trial in criminal cases is, like the right to grand jury indictment, only available for "criminal" charges and not for petty offenses. In analyzing this distinction, the courts focus on the severity of the authorized punishment (State v. Owens; Town of Montclair v. Stanoyevich). In civil cases, the right to jury trial attaches only to matters that, under the common law at the time of the adoption of the constitution, could be submitted to a jury (Chiacchio v. Chiacchio; Ballard v. Schoenberg). The New Jersey Supreme Court has held that modern statutory causes of action under, for example, the law against discrimination, do not require a right to jury trial (Shaner v. Horizon Bancorp.). Legislative implementation of the five-sixths civil jury provision has been upheld (Morin v. Becker).

In criminal cases the jury is an independent decisionmaker with respect to questions of fact on all elements of the criminal charge. Instructions from the trial judge to the jury, however, are an important element of a trial, and the judge may instruct a jury that under certain circumstances it "must" find a defendant guilty (State v. Ragland). Still, the judge may not direct a verdict of guilt (order the jury to find the defendant guilty) in a criminal case (State v. Collier), and a jury may return a verdict of not guilty even in the face of overwhelming evidence of guilt (State v. Ingenito). Ordinarily, appellate courts will not substitute their judgment for that of juries by weighing the evidence on factual questions on appeal (State v. Welsch).

A defendant does not have a right unilaterally to waive a jury trial without prosecution consent or order of the court (State v. Davidson).

RIGHTS OF PERSONS ACCUSED OF CRIME

10. In all criminal prosecutions the accused shall have the right to a speedy and public trial by an impartial jury; to be informed of the nature and cause of the accusation; to be confronted with the witnesses against him; to have compulsory process for obtaining witnesses in his favor; and to have the assistance of counsel in his defense.

This paragraph was carried over verbatim from Article I, section 8, of the 1844 Constitution. Its origins, however, are found in Article XVI of the 1776 Constitution: "That all criminals shall be admitted to the same privileges of witnesses and counsel, as their prosecutors are or shall be entitled to." By the language "the same privileges" the 1776 provision must be taken to refer to such privileges as they existed at common law or under statute at the time. Also, the 1776 provision did not simply freeze prosecution/defense parity at the time of adoption, but made sure to include "are *or shall be entitled* to" (emphasis added) for the apparent purpose of keeping pace with future developments. That goal has now been superseded by the enumeration of rights contained in the current version of paragraph 10. There are numerous rights covered by this provision, but interestingly, the right against self-incrimination is not expressly protected here or elsewhere in the New Jersey Constitution. The doctrine is, however, enforced in New Jersey. See the discussion under Article I, paragraph 21.

Speedy Trial

A defendant's right to a "speedy" trial is intended to protect against unfairness resulting from an undue delay in bringing the defendant to trial. Although it was early held that the right does not attach until a formal criminal charge has been lodged against the defendant (State v. Le Vien), it is now clear that speedy trial rights attach upon arrest (State v. Szima). The question whether a defendant has been denied a speedy trial is analyzed in New Jersey, utilizing federal constitutional doctrine, by balancing four factors: length of delay; the reason for the delay; defendant's expressed desire for a speedy trial; and, prejudice to the defendant because of the delay (State v. Szima; State v. Smith [1976]). In both of these opinions the New Jersey Supreme Court intimated that the state constitutional right may provide *less* protection than the federal Sixth Amendment right to a speedy trial.

Public Trial–Impartial Jury

The rights to a public trial and to trial by an impartial jury are linked together, but sometimes seem contradictory. This is because an open public trial, including pretrial proceedings, which is fully reported in the press, may lead to such pretrial publicity that the defendant may have trouble obtaining an impartial jury—one that has not already formed opinions about the case.

First, New Jersey recognizes the "exceptionally vigorous judicial tradition in this State that favors open judicial proceedings" (State v. Williams). Public trial rights have been held to be violated by a judicial order clearing the courtroom at a sex offense trial (State v. Haskins). At the same time, however, the New Jersey Supreme Court has held that "the triers of fact must be as nearly impartial as the lot of humanity will admit" (State v. Williams). In the Williams case, the Court was able to balance the two rights by setting out guidelines to prevent pretrial publicity that might arise from open pretrial hearings from adversely affecting the defendant's right to an impartial jury. It did not, however, conclude that closure of a trial could never validly be ordered.

In the context of capital cases, the Court has held that neither limiting defendants' questioning of potential jurors on their racial attitudes, nor the process of "death qualifying" the jury (making sure by questioning prior to the trial that jurors will follow the law and impose the death penalty if applicable) deprives a defendant of an impartial jury (State v. Ramseur). Finally, the Court has held that the use of peremptory challenges (the right to dismiss potential jurors without giving any reason) by the prosecution to eliminate minority jurors violates a defendant's right to an impartial jury (State v. Gilmore). Interestingly, the New Jersey Supreme Court rested its decision on the right to an impartial jury, rather than on equal protection analysis such as that used by the U.S. Supreme Court in Batson v. Kentucky in reaching a similar conclusion.

Notice of Charges

As noted with respect to indictments under paragraph 8, criminal complaints must inform a defendant of the charges against him so that he may prepare a defense. This right is also sometimes analyzed as an element of due process of law (State v. Salzman; State in Interest of K.A.W.).

Confrontation of Witnesses

This right is both for the benefit of defendants, so they may cross-examine witnesses against them, and for the benefit of the trier of fact (that is, the judge or jury) to observe the demeanor and appearance of the witnesses so as to determine their credibility. The New Jersey courts have held that the right to confrontation was not violated by a statute permitting videotaped testimony of child witnesses (State v. Bass), and a recent U.S. Supreme Court decision (Coy v. Iowa) striking down a similar statute has been distinguished by the Appellate Division on the ground that the New Jersey statute requires a judicial finding of harm to the minor witness if forced to confront the defendant, whereas that requirement was not present in the statute struck down by the U.S. Supreme Court (State v. Crandall).

Included within the right to confront witnesses is the right of a criminal defendant to be present at all important stages of the criminal trial, including preliminary hearings, unless he voluntarily absents himself (State v. Hardy; State v. Wiggins).

Compulsory Process

Compulsory process (subpoenas or court orders requiring attendance of witnesses at trial) must be provided for defendants (State v. King). This right prevails over the need of the press for confidentiality of sources, but that need will be respected as far as possible (Matter of Farber). Also, the right to compulsory process does not require the state to guarantee the presence of witnesses, particularly those from out of state (State v. Smith [1965]). Finally, the New Jersey Supreme Court has held that a plea agreement in which one defendant agrees not to testify on behalf of a codefendant violates the codefendant's right to compulsory process of witnesses (State v. Fort).

Right to Counsel

This right recognizes the complexity of the legal process, and that "without the guiding hand of counsel, an innocent defendant may lose his freedom because he does not know how to establish his innocence" (State v. Sugar). The New Jersey Supreme Court held in 1971 that indigent defendants should be provided with appointed counsel even in municipal courts, if there was a likelihood of imprisonment "or other consequence of magnitude" (Rodriguez v. Rosenblatt). This holding, however, was not based on the *constitutional* right to counsel, but rather on "considerations of fairness," and "simple justice." Where a defendant claims that assigned counsel's representation was ineffective, the New Jersey Supreme Court has adopted the federal constitutional standard "that if counsel's performance has been so deficient as to create a reasonable probability that those deficiencies materially contributed to defendant's conviction, the constitutional right will have been violated" (State v. Fritz). Finally, not only do defendants have a right to be represented by counsel, but they also have a qualified right to represent themselves at trial. There is a strong presumption, however, against the waiver of the right to counsel, particularly in complex matters like capital cases (State v. Russo).

DOUBLE JEOPARDY; BAIL

11. No person shall, after acquittal, be tried for the same offense. All persons shall, before conviction, be bailable by sufficient sureties, except for capital offenses when the proof is evident or presumption great.

Double Jeopardy

This paragraph was carried over verbatim from Article I, section 10, of the 1844 Constitution. With respect to double jeopardy, it is by its terms ("after acquittal") a more narrow protection for defendants than that provided by the Eighth Amendment to the federal Constitution: "nor shall any person be subject for the same offense to be twice put in jeopardy of life or limb. . . . " In other words, under the federal provision there may be circumstances short of actual *acquittal* that will trigger the federal protection. This distinction in language seems to have been chosen deliberately by the 1844 Constitutional Convention.[15]

Therefore, the federal Fifth Amendment appears to provide broader protection than Article I, paragraph 11 (State v. Rechtschaffer). Although acknowledging this, New Jersey courts have held as recently as 1987 that the federal and state provisions are "co-extensive" (State v. DeLuca). This interpretation of the state and federal provisions as identical means that federal constitutional law on double jeopardy becomes applicable to analysis of the state constitutional right. Therefore, the U.S. Supreme Court's description of federal double jeopardy protection under the Fifth Amendment in North Carolina v. Pierce is apt: "It protects against a second prosecution for the same offense after acquittal. It protects against a second prosecution for the same offense after conviction. And, it protects against multiple punishments for the same offense."

Obviously, the key inquiry under double jeopardy analysis in any of these contexts is whether a successive prosecution is for the "same offense" as was prosecuted earlier. The New Jersey Supreme Court's opinion in State v. DeLuca attempted to resolve the uncertainties by developing a two-pronged test for double jeopardy claims: (1) whether each of the offenses requires proof of an additional fact not necessary for the other offense; or (2) whether proof used to establish guilt in the first prosecution is identical to that used in the second prosecution. The application of this test remains a difficult matter (State v. Yoskowitz).

A question had arisen about the applicability of double jeopardy protections to motor vehicle cases (not, strictly speaking, *criminal* offenses), which the New Jersey courts had kept open by applying the subconstitutional doctrine of "fundamental fairness" rather than constitutional double jeopardy doctrine to such cases (State v. Tropea). This question was recently resolved in State v. Dively, where the New Jersey Supreme Court concluded that under federal interpretations of the Fifth Amendment double jeopardy clause in motor vehicle cases, it was "constrained" to apply double jeopardy principles to motor vehicle cases. Because the New Jersey courts consider state and federal analysis coextensive, this approach raises the question whether an interpretation of the state constitutional provision could be grounded on an adequate and independent ground, insulating the decision from review by the U.S. Supreme Court (Delaware v. Prouse; Michigan v. Long). The Court continues to analyze double jeopardy issues together with the fundamental fairness doctrine (State v. Yoskowitz).

The double jeopardy bar of Article I, paragraph 11 has been held not to prevent a prosecution appeal where a *judge* has entered an acquittal after a jury verdict of guilty (State v. Kleinwaks), nor to bar prosecution appeals of criminal sentences (State v. Jones). When a conviction cannot be obtained because of a failure of proof at trial, as opposed to trial court error, an appellate court may not remand for a new trial (State v. Tropea). Finally, in the context of multiple, as opposed to successive, prosecutions, New Jersey courts have held that "If the accused has committed only one offense, he cannot be punished as if it were two," but have been unable to agree on whether the basis for this protection is double jeopardy, due process, or some other legal protection (State v. Davis; State v. Best; State v. Churchdale Leasing, Inc.).

Bail

Bail is the requirement that a person accused of a crime be permitted to post money or other collateral as a guarantee that he will appear at the trial if released from custody. In contrast to the double jeopardy provision, the bail provision establishes a right to bail that is not included in the Eighth Amendment's prohibition of "excessive bail" (United States v. Salerno). Thus, the right to bail in New Jersey is a basic constitutional right (State v. Johnson [1972]). While the question of *excessive* bail is governed in New Jersey by paragraph 12, this paragraph concerns the underlying right to bail before conviction. Approximately forty other state constitutions contain a similar provision on the right to bail—providing rights beyond those guaranteed in the federal constitution. Because of this state constitutional right to bail, except in capital cases "where the proof is evident or presumption great," any proposal for pretrial preventive detention based on public safety concerns would require a constitutional amendment. Such a proposed amendment was debated and defeated in the New Jersey Legislature in 1986.[16]

After the reimposition of capital punishment in New Jersey, prosecutors may now oppose bail for defendants who are likely to receive the death penalty. This issue will be decided at a bail hearing, at which the state has the burden of showing a reasonable likelihood the death penalty will be imposed. The state may, however, submit evidence that would not be admissible at trial (State v. Engel).

EXCESSIVE BAIL OR FINES; CRUEL AND UNUSUAL PUNISHMENTS

> 12. Excessive bail shall not be required, excessive fines shall not be imposed, and cruel and unusual punishments shall not be inflicted.

This paragraph was carried over verbatim from Article I, section 15, of the 1844 Constitution. It includes protections against three distinct impositions by the government; excessive bail, excessive fines, and cruel and unusual punishments.

Excessive Bail

In addition to the right to bail provided in the preceding paragraph, this provision protects against excessive bail being required of a defendant. Because the matter of setting bail is regulated in detail by rules promulgated by the New Jersey Supreme Court, there is relatively little *constitutional* litigation on the subject of excessive bail. The setting of bail is a highly discretionary function of trial courts, which contemplate the nature of the alleged crime and the character of the defendant, and which will normally be respected by appellate courts (State v. Petrucelli).

Excessive Fines

The limitation on the imposition of excessive fines applies to the legislative branch and to administrative agencies. Normally, the legislature sets an amount of fine or a range within which either a court or administrative agency has discretion to assess a fine. The courts are very deferential to these decisions by the legislature, in the first instance, and to the discretionary impositions of fines by the lower courts and administrative agencies (Department of Community Affairs v. Wertheimer). The Appellate Division has noted that fines, particularly mandatory fines, "alone can amount to cruel and unusual punishment under certain circumstances but the situation is rare" (State in Interest of L. M.). In the L. M. decision, however, the Appellate Division upheld a mandatory one-thousand dollar fine for a juvenile convicted of a drug offense.

Cruel and Unusual Punishment

In interpreting the cruel and unusual clause, the New Jersey Supreme Court has set forth the following test for evaluating punishments: "whether the nature of the criticized punishment shocks the general conscience and violates principles of fundamental fairness; whether comparison shows the punishment to be grossly disproportionate to the offense; and whether the punishment goes beyond what is necessary to accomplish any legitimate penal aim" (State v. DesMarets). The Court has, however, held that the death penalty does not violate this test (State v. Ramseur). In one instance, however, the Court has invalidated the death penalty as applied to a defendant who did not intend to cause death, indicating that "we conclude that Article 1, paragraph 12 of our state constitution . . . affords greater protections to capital defendants than does the eighth amendment of the federal constitution" (State v. Gerald).

IMPRISONMENT FOR DEBT OR MILITIA FINE

13. No person shall be imprisoned for debt in any action, or on any judgment found upon contract, unless in cases of fraud; nor shall any person be imprisoned for a militia fine in time of peace.

This paragraph was carried over verbatim from Article I, section 17, of the 1844 Constitution. It gave constitutional status to the 1842 statutory ban on imprisonment for debt (Perry v. Orr).[17] It contains several guarantees, the most important of which protects persons from imprisonment for debt unless it is accompanied by the criminal offense of fraud. It limits the use of criminal sanctions involving incarceration for civil contractual claims for money (State v. Madewell). Imprisonment for contempt of court, as a means of forcing the payment of money under certain circumstances, however, is not prohibited by this paragraph (Krafte v. Belfus; Aspinwall v. Aspinwall). Further, the capias ad respondendum (where, upon sufficient allegations of fraud, an alleged debtor may be incarcerated until posting a bond adequate to satisfy a judgment) has been held not to violate this provision (Perlmutter v. DeRowe).

HABEAS CORPUS

14. The privilege of the writ of habeas corpus shall not be suspended, unless in case of rebellion or invasion the public safety may require it.

This paragraph was carried over verbatim from Article I, section 11, of the 1844 Constitution and would have been available under the common law adopted by the 1776 Constitution. A writ of habeas corpus is used to challenge in court the lawfulness of a person's incarceration. It is a "collateral" remedy in the sense that it may be used even if the regular avenues of appeal have been exhausted.

Writs of habeas corpus are governed by the Habeas Corpus Act, N.J.S.A. 2A: 67–1. The writ is a flexible and extremely important mechanism for the judicial protection of rights, as recognized by Justice Nathan Jacobs in State v. Cynkowski:

The historic writ of *habeas corpus* is the "precious safeguard of personal liberty" . . . ; it is the only writ which is preserved *eo nomine* in our *State Constitution* (Article I, par. 14), and our courts are rightly fervent to insure that it is ever available for the protection of the accused, whatever be his station.

MILITARY SUBORDINATE TO CIVIL POWER

15. The military shall be in strict subordination to the civil power.

This paragraph was carried over verbatim from Article I, section 12, of the 1844 Constitution. The principle was implicit in Article VIII of the 1776 Constitution providing that the governor was "commander-in-chief of all the militia, and other military force in this colony. . . . " These constitutional statements express a fundamental tenet of American constitutionalism, originating at least as early as 1776. The current provision has not been the subject of judicial interpretation.

QUARTERING OF SOLDIERS

> 16. No soldier shall, in time of peace, be quartered in any house, without the consent of the owner; nor in time of war, except in a manner prescribed by law.

This paragraph was carried over verbatim from Article I, section 13, of the 1844 Constitution. It has not been the subject of judicial interpretation.

TREASON

> 17. Treason against the State shall consist only in levying war against it, or in adhering to its enemies, giving them aid and comfort. No person shall be convicted of treason, unless on the testimony of two witnesses to the same overt act, or on confession in open court.

This paragraph was carried over verbatim from Article I, section 14, of the 1844 Constitution. It is the only provision in the constitution that defines a criminal offense, and it appears that the legislature may not expand it through broader definitions of treason or sedition (Colgan v. Sullivan).

RIGHT OF ASSEMBLY AND PETITION

> 18. The people have the right freely to assemble together, to consult for the common good, to make known their opinions to their representatives, and to petition for redress of grievances.

This paragraph was carried over verbatim from Article I, section 18, of the 1844 Constitution. It must be considered together with paragraph 6 because the New Jersey Constitution treats freedom of speech and press (paragraph 6) in a separate provision from freedom of assembly and petition (paragraph 18). This approach is different from the First Amendment to the federal Constitution, which treats freedom of speech, press, and assembly all together.

The right to assemble and petition, like the paragraph 6 right to free speech and press is an *affirmative* right. In other words, it dose not simply limit what government may do, but actually grants rights to persons that may be enforceable against persons and entities who are not part of the government (State v. Schmid).

With respect to the time, place, and manner of assembly, the right to assemble and petition is subject to reasonable governmental regulation (Camarco v. City of Orange; Anderson v. Sills).

PERSONS IN PRIVATE EMPLOYMENT; RIGHT TO ORGANIZE; COLLECTIVE BARGAINING; PUBLIC EMPLOYEES

> 19. Persons in private employment shall have the right to organize and bargain collectively. Persons in public employment shall have the right to organize, present to and make known to the State, or any of its political subdivisions or agencies, their grievances and proposals through representatives of their own choosing.

This paragraph was added to Article I by the 1947 Constitutional Convention.[18] The provision grants broader rights to private employees than to public employees (Lullo v. Int'l. Assn. of Firefighters; Ridgefield Park Educ. Assoc. v. Ridgefield Park Board of Ed.). Private employees are guaranteed the right to "organize and bargain collectively." Public employees are entitled to organize, but they only have the right to "present and make known . . . their grievances and proposals." Currently, because legislation has been enacted governing labor relations in the public sector, in that field the constitutional provision has been to a large extent supplanted by the statutory provisions. Therefore, most questions concerning the details of public employees' rights are resolved in the context of applying these statutes. The courts have interpreted this provision to prohibit strikes by public employees (Delaware River and Bay Authority v. International Organization of Masters, Mates and Pilots).

The Supreme Court of New Jersey has consistently and unambiguously held that state courts have jurisdiction over claims asserted under this provision and that it is a valid, self-executing, legal basis for a cause of action alleging interference with the rights to organize and bargain collectively even in the absence of statutory law authorizing such suits (Independent Dairy Workers Union v. Milk Drivers & Dairy Employees Local 680).

In Johnson v. Christ Hospital, the Chancery Division interpreted paragraph 19 as imposing an affirmative duty upon an employer to bargain collectively with employees or their representatives. In support of its construction, the court quoted extensively from a dialogue in a committee hearing between witness Thomas Parsonnet and a convention delegate, Judge Robert Carey, in which Parsonnet contended that unless the constitution contained a positive statement of the right to bargain collectively, employees would not be able to resort to the courts to compel such bargaining.

In cases involving private employees, because there is no statutory regulation of labor relations in the private sector, New Jersey courts have developed a body of judge-made labor law. New Jersey decisions in both the public and private sectors draw upon federal labor law doctrines (In re Bridgewater Twp.) which, although "helpful," are "in no sense binding" (Cooper v. Nutley Sun Printing Co., Inc.). The courts have enforced Article I, paragraph 19, with respect to a wide range of traditional labor law issues (Comite Organizador de Trabajadores Agricolas (COTA) v. Molinelli).

PRIVATE PROPERTY FOR PUBLIC USE

20. Private property shall not be taken for public use without just compensation. Individuals or private corporations shall not be authorized to take private property for public use without just compensation first made to the owners.

This paragraph had its textual origin in Article I, section 16, and Article IV, section 7, paragraph 9 (renumbered paragraph 8 by an 1875 amendment), of the 1844 Constitution. The principles it states, however, originated in the judicially enforced doctrine of vested rights that grew up under the 1776 Constitution.[19] The right to just compensation for property taken for public use has a close relationship to the doctrine that property may not be taken without due process of law. Just as the 1844 constitution, the current constitution has two provisions on just compensation: this paragraph, and Article IV, Section VI, paragraph 3, which deals with acquisition of private property by state or local government. See the discussion under that provision.

The current provision recognizes that as part of its sovereign power, the government may take private property for public uses and that this power may even be delegated to individuals or private corporations. It limits that power, however, by requiring that "just compensation" be paid for the property (State by State Highway Commissioner, v. Burnett). With respect to takings of property by individuals or corporations, pursuant to government authorization, the provision specifically requires the compensation be "first made" to the owners. This extra requirement, added by the 1844 Constitution, was held not to apply retroactively to corporations chartered before 1844 and authorized to take property without "first" paying compensation (Lehigh Valley Railway Co. v. McFarlan).

The taking of private property for public use, referred to as condemnation, or, the power of eminent domain, is subject to complex statutory regulation, and the notion of "just compensation" can be complicated, as can the concept of a "taking" of property and "public use."

Property may not be taken through the power of eminent domain to be put to private use; the only justification for use of the power is where the property is to be put to some public use (State by State Highway Commissioner v. Totowa Lumber and Supply Co.). "Just compensation" is a flexible concept, which will vary depending on the circumstances of individual cases, with due deference to legislative judgments. The New Jersey Supreme Court has stated: "The provision of the Constitution for the payment of just compensation is primarily a restriction on the power of the Legislature for the benefit of the property owner. As we have said, it is not a specific measuring rule and there is a margin of discretion for the courts and the Legislature in devising rules to insure such compensation'' (Jersey City Redevelopment Agency v. Kugler).

A "taking" can be accomplished by a wide variety of indirect methods, such as severe land use regulation. Government, however, has broad authority to regulate, for the health, safety, and welfare of the community under its police power, and the exercise of such power will not be considered a "taking" of someone's property unless it is "confiscatory" (Matter of Egg Harbor Associates (Bayshore Center); Lom-Ran Corp. v. Department of Environmental Protection). The New Jersey Supreme Court has stated that "restrictions on land use short of total appropriation, if sufficiently extensive and prolonged, may constitute a taking" (Schiavone Construction Co. v. Hakensack Meadowlands Development Commission). This sort of indirect taking is often referred to as inverse condemnation. Also, under limited circumstances, certain "pretaking" activities by the government that deprive a landowner of all use of his property can be considered a taking. The New Jersey Supreme Court has held, however, that preliminary identification of land as a potential hazardous waste facility site, even though interfering with the landowner's development opportunities, does not constitute a taking (Littman v. Gimello).

SAVING CLAUSE

> 21. This enumeration of rights and privileges shall not be construed to impair or deny others retained by the people.

This paragraph was carried over verbatim from Article I, section 19, of the 1844 Constitution. The "saving clause" was not contained in the original draft of the Bill of Rights, but rather was added at the insistence of Chief Justice Joseph C. Hornblower, a delegate.[20] Hornblower reportedly said:

Now, this bill of rights don't contain half our rights and he did not want those not expressed to be excluded. If they were all expressed they would be as long as the moral law—or the five books of Moses. He moved therefore to add a saving clause, to the effect that this bill of rights shall not abridge or take away any natural rights which are not here enumerated.[21]

Although at first blush this clause may appear to have no important content, this may not be the case. In a 1951 decision, State v. Labato, the Supreme Court seemed to consider Article I, paragraph 21 as a vehicle for recognizing rights that were protected at common law. This case dealt with double jeopardy, a right that is expressly covered under paragraph 11, but only to the extent of protecting persons "after acquittal." Labato had been earlier *convicted* of a violation of the Disorderly Persons Act in police court and was later indicted for a crime based on the same offense. Therefore, his plea of double jeopardy did not come under the plain language of paragraph 11. Further, this case arose before federal double jeopardy protections were applied to the states (Benton v. Maryland). The Court noted "But the enumeration of 'rights and privileges' in this article of the Constitution 'shall not be construed to impair or deny others retained by the people.' " The Court went on to note that the right not to be retried after conviction was protected by the common law, dating back to the Magna Charta.

The Labato case has been referred to by a commentator as illustrating the "right-protective approach" to interpreting unenumerated rights clauses in state constitutions. In other words, the clause can be viewed as protecting important rights, historically viewed as fundamental, even though they are not enumerated.[22] A proper analysis of arguments under this approach would have to focus on the few rights specified in the 1776 Constitution, together with rights under the common law, which was adopted by Article XXII of the 1776 New Jersey Constitution.

Article I, paragraph 21, may therefore provide a constitutional vehicle for protecting rights not expressly covered by the state constitution. A good example is the "right" against self-incrimination, which is not expressly protected by the New Jersey Constitution. However, as Justice William J. Brennan, Jr., noted in State v. Fary in 1955:

Although not written into our State Constitution (as it is in the Fifth Amendment to the Federal Constitution and in the constitutions of all our sister states except Iowa), and not given even statutory expression until it appeared as section 4 of the Evidence Act of 1855 ... the privilege has been firmly established in New Jersey since our beginnings as a State.

Although Justice Brennan did not cite Article I, paragraph 21, it could have provided a valid constitutional underpinning for his view. More recent New Jersey Supreme Court decisions consider state self-incrimination doctrine, although broader than federal constitutional doctrine, to be a matter to be treated under the common law and the rules of evidence (State v. Hartley; In re Martin; State v. Deatore; In re Grand Jury Proceedings of Guarino).

Article II

Elections and Suffrage

1. General elections shall be held annually on the first Tuesday after the first Monday in November; but the time of holding such elections may be altered by law. The Governor and members of the Legislature shall be chosen at general elections. Local elective officers shall be chosen at general elections or at such other times as shall be provided by law.

This article on elections and suffrage has its origins in the Constitution of 1776, although it was an 1875 amendment that first established the November date for elections.

This current provision maintains the format of setting a date for general elections in the constitution, but permitting alteration by the legislature. It mandates that members of the legislature and the governor be chosen at general elections and that local officials may be chosen at general elections or otherwise as provided by the legislature.

When a question arose as to whether the legislature could regulate *primary* elections, to choose the nominees of the political parties, the Supreme Court upheld such legislative regulation, noting "The same public interest is advanced in the regulation of the selective mechanism as in the protection of general elections" (Wene v. Meyner).

2. All questions submitted to the people of the entire State shall be voted upon at the general election next occurring at least 70 days following the final action of the Governor or the Legislature, as appropriate, necessary to submit the questions. The text of any such question shall be published at least once in one or more newspapers of each county, if any newspapers be published therein, at least 60 days before the election at which it is to be

submitted to the people, and the results of the vote upon a question shall be void unless the text thereof shall have been so published.

This paragraph makes the policy choice that "ballot propositions" or referenda of various types must be voted on at general, rather than primary or special elections. Such referenda would include those on proposed state constitutional amendments, authorizing certain borrowing, approval of forms of gambling, and so forth. The 1844 Constitution, in its cumbersome amendment procedure, required that proposed constitutional amendments be voted on "at a special election to be held for that purpose only." Under the 1844 document, voting on debts in excess of $100,000 was to be at general elections.

This paragraph must be read in conjunction with paragraphs 3, 4, and 5 of Article IX, relating to the submission of proposed constitutional amendments to the electorate.

Prior to 1988, this paragraph contained only the requirement of a general election vote. The additional requirements were added in 1988 to make certain that adequate time and public notice were required prior to the general election vote. These requirements are backed up by the sanction of invalidating the vote when the requirements are not followed.

> 3. (a) Every citizen of the United States, of the age of 18 years, who shall have been a resident of this State and of the country in which he claims his vote 30 days, next before the election, shall be entitled to vote for all officers that now are or hereafter may be elective by the people, and upon all questions which may be submitted to a vote of the people; and
>
> (b) (Deleted by amendment, effective December 5, 1974.)

This paragraph governs the extremely important matter of qualifications for the constitutional right to vote, placing them "beyond legislative curtailment" (Strothers v. Martini).[23] The right to vote is one of the most fundamental of all constitutional rights. In the words of the New Jersey Supreme Court in Asbury Park Press, Inc. v. Wolley:

Ours is a representative form of government. It can remain such in the true sense only if the vote of each citizen has equality with that of his neighbor in the other counties of the State, according to the prescription of the organic law. . . . No man can boast of a higher privilege than the right granted to the citizens of our State and Nation of equal suffrage and thereby to equal representation in the making of the laws of the land. Under our *Constitution* that right is absolute. It is one of which he cannot be deprived, either deliberately or by inaction on the part of a Legislature.

Article IV of the 1776 Constitution provided that "all inhabitants of this Colony, of full age, who are worth fifty pounds" and met a twelve-month residency test could vote. It was this provision that supported voting by women and blacks in New Jersey, long before any other state, from 1790 until 1807. The 1844 Constitution, however, restricted the vote to "white male citizen[s]."

The word "white" was deleted from the paragraph in an 1875 amendment. The current provision reflects a series of further amendments over the years reducing the required residency period and, in 1974, recognizing voting for eighteen-year-olds. The phrase "shall be entitled to vote for all officers that now are or hereafter may be elective by the people" has been held to bar a statutory provision limiting voters to voting for only two candidates for three seats on a statutorily created local government commission (Humble Oil and Refining Co. v. Wojtycha), and from restricting the franchise to freeholders, even for a statutorily created road commission (Allison v. Blake). Such entitlement, however, does not extend to permit a registered party member to vote in another party's "closed" primary election (Smith v. Penta). In other respects, however, the right to vote in primary elections is generally protected under this constitutional provision (Quaremba v. Allan; Smith v. Penta).

In 1972 the Supreme Court held that college students who were bona fide residents of college communities could vote in local elections (Worden v. Mercer County Board of Elections). Even though this result was clearly required under federal law by 1972, the Court specifically adopted the federal "compelling state interest test in its broadest aspects . . . for purposes of our own state constitution and legislation." Interestingly, as the Court noted, there had been a lively discussion in the 1844 Constitutional Convention concerning an unsuccessful proposal to exclude from voting "students who had taken up a transient residence for the purpose of education."

Although the right to vote is a constitutional right, the legislature may introduce reasonable regulation of that right, such as the requirement of registration, so long as "the constitutional qualifications of electors" are not "enlarged by the lawmaking authority" (Gangemi v. Berry).

> (c) Any person registered as a voter in any election district of this State who has removed or shall remove to another state or to another county within this State and is not able there to qualify to vote by reason of an insufficient period of residence in such state or county, shall, as a citizen of the United States, have the right to vote for electors for President and Vice President of the United States, only, by Presidential Elector Absentee Ballot, in the county from which he has removed, in such manner as the Legislature shall provide.

This subparagraph was new in 1947. It provides that if a registered voter in New Jersey moves either out of state or to another election district elsewhere in New Jersey, and a federal presidential election takes place before the voter qualifies by period of residence to vote in the new state or election district, he may vote by absentee ballot for president and vice president in the old election district. This preserves the right to vote in federal presidential elections even for those persons who have moved so recently as not to qualify to vote at their new place of residence. The provision has not been the subject of judicial interpretation.

> 4. In time of war no elector in the military service of the State or in the armed forces of the United States shall be deprived of his vote by reason of absence from his election district. The Legislature may provide for absentee voting by members of the armed forces of the United States in time of peace. The Legislature may provide the manner in which and the time and place at which such absent electors may vote, and for the return and canvass of their votes in the election district in which they respectively reside.

The guarantee to military personnel of the right to vote during wartime was added by amendment in 1875. The specific 1947 authorization of legislation providing for absentee voting by members of the armed services in time of peace was relied upon in a challenge to legislative provision for absentee voting by *civilians*. The Supreme Court noted the differing treatment of absentee voting during peacetime and wartime in Gangemi v. Berry:

> The 1947 Constitution does not in terms affirmatively prohibit civilian absentee voting; and the purpose so to do is not revealed as a matter of negative inference. The preceding *paragraph* 3 of *Article* II of the Constitution insures the right of suffrage to every citizen of the given age and residence qualifications. In regard to absentee voting, *paragraph* 4 treats electors absent in military service as in the one category, but differently as to imperative right depending upon whether the military service is rendered in time of war or in time of peace. In the former case, there is an absolute right to vote, constitutionally secured against legislative impairment, as was so under the 1844 Constitution; in the latter, the Legislature "may provide" for such absentee voting, a provision not expressly incorporated in the 1844 Constitution, perhaps deemed advisable in view of the general residence suffrage requirements of *paragraph* 3.

The Court went on to conclude, after tracing the history of the provisions, that the constitutional provision permitting the legislature to provide for absentee voting by those in the military during peacetime, could not, through "negative implication," preclude the legislature from permitting civilians to vote by absentee ballot.[24]

> 5. No person in the military, naval or marine service of the United States shall be considered a resident of this State by being stationed in any garrison, barrack, or military or naval place or station within this State.

This provision appeared first in Article II, paragraph 1, of the 1844 Constitution and was carried over in the 1947 Constitution. It purports to create an exception to the paragraph 3 guarantee of voting rights, but despite its apparently clear language, it is of questionable validity under federal law. A 1972 Law Division opinion, relying heavily on a U.S. Supreme Court decision invalidating a similar provision of the Texas Constitution, concluded that the provision could not be applied to bar a resident on a military base who met the residency requirements of paragraph 3 from voting (New Hanover Township v. Kelly).

> 6. No idiot or insane person shall enjoy the right of suffrage.

This operates as an exception to the paragraph 3 guarantee of voting rights. The words ''idiot'' and ''insane'' are, of course, imprecise and have received no satisfactory definition. The Appellate Division held that persons who are mentally retarded and receiving residential services at the New Lisbon State School do not automatically meet these definitions for exclusion from the constitutional right to vote (Carroll v. Cobb).

> 7. The Legislature may pass laws to deprive persons of the right of suffrage who shall be convicted of such crimes as it may designate. Any person so deprived, when pardoned or otherwise restored by law to the right of suffrage, shall again enjoy that right.

This permits the legislature to, if it chooses, make exceptions to the paragraph 3 guarantee of voting rights. The provision has its origins in paragraphs 1 and 2 of Article II of the 1844 Constitution, which were the subject of considerable debate at the 1844 Convention.

The legislature implemented this paragraph by statute (N.J.S.A. 19:4–1). Its choice of crimes that would result in disenfranchisement was declared in violation of the federal Constitution's equal protection clause in 1970 (Stephens v. Yeomans). Generally speaking, questions of voter eligibility under this provision turn on questions of statutory, rather than constitutional, interpretation (Hitchner v. Cumberland County Board of Elections).

Article III

Distribution of the Powers of Government

1. The powers of the government shall be divided among three distinct branches, the legislative, executive, and judicial. No person or persons belonging to or constituting one branch shall exercise any of the powers properly belonging to either of the others, except as expressly provided in this Constitution.

In this provision, first inserted as Article III in the Constitution in 1844, New Jersey provides an express, textual statement of the separation of powers doctrine. This must be contrasted with the federal Constitution and a number of other state constitutions, where the doctrine is only implied from the creation of, and assignment of powers to, the three branches of government. By including an express separation of powers provision, New Jersey followed a model dating back to the 1776 Virginia and the 1780 Massachusetts constitutions.[25]

In contrast to courts in some other states, however, New Jersey courts do not seem to attribute any special significance to the fact that the separation of powers doctrine is expressed textually in the constitution rather than merely implied.[26] The Supreme Court noted in Brown v. Heymann:

There is no indication that our State Constitution was intended, with respect to the delegation of legislative power, to depart from the basic concept of distribution of the powers of government embodied in the Federal Constitution. It seems evident that in this regard the design spelled out in our State Constitution would be implied in constitutions which are not explicit in this regard. . . . We have heretofore said our State Constitution is "no more restrictive" in this respect than the Federal Constitution. . . . Indeed in our State the judiciary has accepted delegations of legislative power which probably exceed federal experience.

To analyze separation of powers problems, the starting point is understanding the distinctions between legislative (Article IV, Section I, paragraph 1), executive (Article V, Section I, paragraph 1) and judicial (Article VI, Section I, paragraph 1) powers. These are, in many instances, difficult to distinguish, and there is significant blurring as one approaches the dividing lines. Furthermore, problems arise both from attempted encroachments of one branch on another and also from attempts by one branch to give up its powers, as in the context of unlawful delegation of legislative power. Separation of powers restrictions protect the "essential integrity" of each branch, but should not be interpreted so as to prevent cooperative actions by two or more branches (Gilbert v. Gladden). Also, the last clause in the provision: "except as expressly provided in this Constitution" indicates that there are express exceptions throughout the rest of the Constitution, to the separation of powers doctrine (Ross v. Board of Chosen Freeholders of Essex County). A clear example of such an express exception is Article V, Section I, paragraph 6, providing that the president of the Senate shall serve as governor in the event of a vacancy in that office. Under such circumstances, the governor/president of the Senate may even continue to exercise legislative duties (Ackerman Dairy, Inc. v. Kandle).

The constitutional separation of powers doctrine is not applicable to local governments (Smith v. Hazlet Township; Eggers v. Kenny).

In upholding the Law Against Discrimination against a charge that it unconstitutionally vested the power to adjudicate in an executive agency, the Supreme Court noted in David v. Vesta Co.:

The doctrine of separation of powers must therefore be viewed not as an end in itself, but as a general principle intended to be applied so as to maintain the balance between the three branches of government, to preserve their respective independence and integrity, and prevent the concentration of *unchecked* power in the hands of any one branch.

In upholding the legislature's creation of the State Commission of Investigation, the Court rejected separation of powers challenges to the legislative commission despite the fact that the governor appointed some of its members and could request investigations, concluding that the "power to investigate reposes in all three branches" (Zicarelli v. New Jersey State Commission of Investigation). The Court did, however, strike down a "legislative veto" mechanism on the ground that it encroached on executive power by purporting to make law without presentment to the governor for a possible veto (General Assembly v. Byrne; Enourato v. New Jersey Building Authority). But, the New Jersey courts are extremely liberal in permitting legislative delegations to the executive branch, often noting the requirement of proper legislative standards to guide administrative discretion, while upholding the delegation under review (Township of Mt. Laurel v. Department of the Public Advocate). The Supreme Court has upheld expansive use of its own rulemaking power against separation of powers challenges (State v. Leonardis; Busik v. Levine).

Article IV

Legislative

SECTION I

1. The legislative power shall be vested in a Senate and General Assembly.

The legislative article of the constitution establishes the legislative branch, assigns it the "legislative power," provides for methods of choosing representatives and structuring legislative processes, and provides limits on and certain grants of legislative power. This first paragraph of Section I establishes a bicameral or two-house legislature, a model that, with few exceptions, is a basic element of American constitutionalism. Under the state's first constitution the upper house was called the "Legislative Council," but this was reformulated in the 1844 Constitution and renamed the senate. A number of the amendments adopted in 1875 were to the legislative article.

It is important to distinguish state legislative power from federal legislative power. As the New Jersey Supreme Court has said in *Gangemi v. Berry*:

The legislative authority in the States consists of "the full and complete power as it rests in, and may be exercised by, the sovereign power of any country, subject only to such restrictions as [the people] may have seen fit to impose, and to the limitations which are contained in the Constitution of the United States," and the legislative department "is not made a special agency for the exercise of specifically defined legislative powers, but is entrusted with the general authority to make laws at discretion."

Because of this basic, plenary quality of state legislative power, much of the rest of the legislative article contains limitations on this broad legislative power.

The central feature of plenary state legislative authority is the "police power," which justifies legislation to further the public health, safety, welfare, and morals. This power, however, may not be invoked "solely for the economic protection of particular individuals and groups . . . where the dominant purpose of legislation is to advance private interests under the guise of the general welfare" (Independent Electricians and Electrical Contractors' Association v. New Jersey Board of Examiners of Electrical Contractors). Every presumption, however, will be accorded by the New Jersey courts to a statute challenged as an invalid exercise of the police power (Matter of C.V.S. Pharmacy). The New Jersey Supreme Court has stated that the police power is so fundamental that it "does not have its genesis in a written constitution. It is an essential element of the social compact, an attribute of sovereignty itself, possessed by the states before the adoption of the Federal Constitution" (Rosselle v. Wright).

The legislative power includes the broad, but not unlimited power of investigation into subjects that may require legislation (In re Zicarelli). Furthermore, the legislature may delegate its power to administrative agencies so long as it provides adequate standards (including those that may be inferred) to protect against arbitrary agency action (Sheeran v. Nationwide Mutual Insurance Co., Inc.). As indicated in the discussion of Article III, New Jersey recognizes a very liberal standard, permitting broad delegations of legislative power.

In deference to legislative authority, New Jersey courts accord legislative enactments a strong presumption of constitutionality (Hutton Park Gardens v. West Orange Town Council). The New Jersey Supreme Court has ruled, however, that state legislation may not be applied to an agency created by an interstate compact between New Jersey and Pennsylvania, the Delaware River Port Authority (Eastern Paralyzed Veterans Association, Inc. v. City of Camden).

> 2. No person shall be a member of the Senate who shall not have attained the age of thirty years, and have been a citizen and resident of the State for four years, and of the district for which he shall be elected one year, next before his election. No person shall be a member of the General Assembly who shall not have attained the age of twenty-one years and have been a citizen and resident of the State for two years, and of the district for which he shall be elected one year, next before his election. No person shall be eligible for membership in the Legislature unless he be entitled to the right of suffrage.

This provision sets the eligibility requirements for holding a seat in the legislature. The 1776 document contained no minimum age requirements, and their inclusion in the 1844 Constitution generated spirited debate. Article IV, section 1, paragraph 2, of the 1844 Constitution was virtually identical to the current version, except for the 1966 amendment that changed the words "county" to "district" to reflect that year's major revision of the basis for apportionment.

In 1976 the Supreme Court upheld the age restrictions for legislative office against a federal constitutional equal protection challenge, concluding: "classifications based on residence, age, and citizenship are expressive of the state's legitimate interest in the integrity of the ballot, and if these classifications are reasonable, they are constitutionally inoffensive'' (Wurtzel v. Falcey). Justice Pashman filed a lone dissent, stating, ''The age requirements of *N.J. Constitution* (1947), Article IV, Section I, paragraph 2, represent manifestations of by-gone days which fail to comport with reality.''

An opinion of the New Jersey attorney general provides authoritative advice on the exact points in time at which candidates must meet each of the eligibility requirements (Formal Opinion of the Attorney General, No. 5 [Feb. 26, 1980]).

The Supreme Court, as a general matter, has upheld legislative or common-law restrictions on legislators' ''activities extraneous to the office of legislator'' (Reilly v. Ozzard).

> 3. Each Legislature shall be constituted for a term of 2 years beginning at noon on the second Tuesday in January in each even numbered year, at which time the Senate and General Assembly shall meet and organize separately and the first annual session of the Legislature shall commence. Said first annual session shall terminate at noon on the second Tuesday in January next following, at which time the second annual session shall commence and it shall terminate at noon on the second Tuesday in January then next following but either session may be sooner terminated by adjournment sine die. All business before either House or any of the committees thereof at the end of the first annual session may be resumed in the second annual session. The legislative year shall commence at noon on the second Tuesday in January of each year.

This paragraph, as amended in 1968 to take effect in 1970, basically provides for a continuing two-year session of the legislature, with legislative business carrying over from the first annual session to the second annual session.

Such a provision was unnecessary under the 1776 Constitution which specified *annual* legislative elections (Art. III). The 1844 Constitution, in Article IV, section 1, paragraph 3, continued annual elections for the general assembly, with a single legislative year. The courts ruled that, under the 1844 Constitution, neither the house nor the senate were ''continuing bodies'' (Werts v. Rogers; In re Hague).

> 4. Special sessions of the Legislature shall be called by the Governor upon petition of a majority of all the members of each house, and may be called by the Governor whenever in his opinion the public interest shall require.

This paragraph, together with Article V, Section I, paragraph 12, governs the calling of special sessions of the legislature. The governor *must* call a special session when petitioned by a majority of both houses, and *may* do so when ''in his opinion the public interest shall require.''

Article V of the 1776 Constitution permitted the assembly "to empower their Speaker to convene them, whenever any extraordinary occurrence shall render it necessary." Under Article VI the governor was required to convene the council (upper house) whenever the assembly was in session. There was no equivalent of this paragraph in the legislative article of the 1844 Constitution, but the executive article, Article V, paragraph 6, stated that "he shall have power to convene the legislature whenever in his opinion public necessity requires it." This current paragraph in the legislative article was added in 1947.

The courts have held that the governor may call one house into special session during the time it is in regular session but in interim adjournment, concluding that this action is not the calling of a "special session" under this paragraph (Application of Lamb).

SECTION II

Sections II and III of Article IV are the product of the 1966 Constitutional Convention, called to respond to the New Jersey Supreme Court's 1964 Jackman v. Bodine decision declaring the New Jersey apportionment scheme unconstitutional in the wake of the U.S. Supreme Court's one-person-one-vote decisions. The Court concluded that a constitutional convention had to be convened, without a vote of the people on whether it should be called to deal with the crisis.[27] Thus began the Court's deep involvement in reapportionment issues over the next decade.[28]

> 1. The Senate shall be composed of forty senators apportioned among Senate districts as nearly as may be according to the number of their inhabitants as reported in the last preceding decennial census of the United States and according to the method of equal proportions. Each Senate district shall be composed, wherever practicable, of one single county, and, if not so practicable, of two or more contiguous whole counties.

This paragraph, the product of the 1966 Constitutional Convention on reapportionment, finally brought an end to the equal representation of counties in the senate. It establishes a forty-member senate.

Following the 1970 census, the New Jersey Supreme Court ruled that this paragraph's attempt to use counties as the "building blocks" for senatorial districts, in light of the federal constitutional one-person-one-vote requirement, could not be enforced (Davenport v. Apportionment Commission). The Court recognized the internal conflict between the preservation of county lines and "as nearly as may be according to the number of their inhabitants" (Scrimminger v. Sherwin). Although "compactness" is not specifically required for Senate districts as it is for assembly districts (Article IV, Section II, paragraph 3), it is required for both by the courts (Davenport v. Apportionment Commission).

2. Each Senator shall be elected by the legally qualified voters of the Senate district, except that if the Senate district is composed of two or more counties and two senators are apportioned to the district, one senator shall be elected by the legally qualified voters of each Assembly district. Each senator shall be elected for a term beginning at noon of the second Tuesday in January next following his election and ending at noon of the second Tuesday in January four years thereafter, except that each senator, to be elected for a term beginning in January of the second year following the year in which a decennial census of the United States is taken, shall be elected for a term of two years.

This paragraph, also dating from 1966, links senatorial districts with two senators to assembly districts. Further, it establishes a four-year term for senators, except for the two-year term right after each decennial census.

3. The General Assembly shall be composed of eighty members. Each Senate district to which only one senator is apportioned shall constitute an Assembly district. Each of the remaining Senate districts shall be divided into Assembly districts equal in number to the number of senators apportioned to the Senate district. The Assembly districts shall be composed of contiguous territory, as nearly compact and equal in the number of their inhabitants as possible, and in no event shall each such district contain less than eighty percent nor more than one hundred twenty percent of one-fortieth of the total number of inhabitants of the State as reported in the last preceding decennial census of the United States. Unless necessary to meet the foregoing requirements, no county or municipality shall be divided among Assembly districts unless it shall contain more than one-fortieth of the total number of inhabitants of the State, and no county or municipality shall be divided among a number of Assembly districts larger than one plus the whole number obtained by dividing the number of inhabitants in the county or municipality by one-fortieth of the total number of inhabitants of the State.

This paragraph, also dating from 1966, creates an eighty-member assembly. Its reference to municipal boundaries has been cited in support of the permissible use of municipalities as "building blocks" for creation of assembly districts (Scrimminger v. Sherwin). The New Jersey Supreme Court has ruled that, despite this provision's basic technique of allocating two assemblymen to each senate district, the assembly must be apportioned according to the equal proportions method (Jackman v. Bodine [1967]; Jackman v. Bodine [1970]). "Compactness" must be observed in constructing districts, but it may be tempered by the concept of "political fairness," which balances political party strength and protects incumbents (Davenport v. Apportionment Commission). The "outer limit" of numerical deviations among districts provided in this paragraph, although not "inherently intolerable" (Jackman v. Bodine [1970]), does not in itself justify any deviation without a demonstrated important reason (Jackman v. Bodine [1967]).

4. Two members of the General Assembly shall be elected by the legally qualified voters of each Assembly district for terms beginning at noon of the second Tuesday in January next following their election and ending at noon of the second Tuesday in January two years thereafter.

This paragraph, also dating from 1966, establishes a two-year assembly term. It has not been the subject of judicial interpretation.

SECTION III

1. After the next and every subsequent decennial census of the United States, the Senate districts and Assembly districts shall be established, and the senators and members of the General Assembly shall be apportioned among them, by an Apportionment Commission consisting of ten members, five to be appointed by the chairman of the State committee of each of the two political parties whose candidates for Governor receive the largest number of votes at the most recent gubernatorial election. Each State chairman, in making such appointments, shall give due consideration to the representation of the various geographical areas of the State. Appointments to the Commission shall be made on or before November 15 of the year in which such census is taken and shall be certified by the Secretary of State on or before December 1 of that year. The Commission, by a majority of the whole number of its members, shall certify the establishment of Senate and Assembly districts and the apportionment of senators and members of the General Assembly to the Secretary of State within one month of the receipt by the Governor of the official decennial census of the United States for New Jersey, or on or before February 1 of the year following the year in which the census is taken, whichever date is later.

This provision, also dating from 1966, is designed to take the intensely political matter of reapportionment out of the hands of the legislature, and assign it to an apportionment commission.[29] Therefore, it is now the commission, not the legislature, which adopts reapportionment plans and whose product is reviewed by the courts. The New Jersey Supreme Court has said, with respect to commission plans, that the "judicial role in reviewing the validity of such a plan is limited" (Davenport v. Apportionment Commission). The commission, established in 1966 in the "Schedule," Article XI, Section V (authorizing the chief justice to appoint an eleventh member) played a major role in implementing the one-person-one-vote mandate.

2. If the Apportionment Commission fails so to certify such establishment and apportionment to the Secretary of State on or before the date fixed or if prior thereto it determines that it will be unable so to do, it shall so certify to the Chief Justice of the Supreme Court of New Jersey and he shall appoint an eleventh member of the Commission. The Commission so constituted, by a majority of the whole number of its members, shall, within one month

after the appointment of such eleventh member, certify to the Secretary of
State the establishment of Senate and Assembly districts and the apportionment of senators and members of the General Assembly.

This paragraph, also dating from 1966, provides a mechanism for resolving
an impasse in the ten-member commission. The appointment of the eleventh
member was instrumental in the interim efforts of the commission to implement
the one-person-one-vote mandates. Even then, however, the Supreme Court had
to step in to solve an immediate post-election districting problem in 1967 (Jackman v. Bodine [1967]).

3. Such establishment and apportionment shall be used thereafter for the
election of members of the Legislature and shall remain unaltered until the
following decennial census of the United States for New Jersey shall have
been received by the Governor.

This paragraph, also dating from 1966, establishes the commission's product
as the valid apportionment scheme until the next decennial census. Therefore,
any legislative attempt at reapportionment would be invalid. The provision has
not been the subject of judicial interpretation.

SECTION IV

1. Any vacancy in the Legislature occasioned otherwise than by expiration
of term shall be filled by election for the unexpired term only at the next
general election occurring not less than 51 days after the occurrence of the
vacancy, except that no vacancy shall be filled at the general election which
immediately precedes the expiration of the term in which the vacancy occurs.
For the interim period pending the election and qualification of a successor
to fill the vacancy, or for the remainder of the term in the case of a vacancy
occurring which cannot be filled pursuant to the terms of this paragraph at
the general election, the vacancy shall be filled within 35 days by the
members of the county committee of the political party of which the incum-
bent was the nominee from the municipalities or districts or units thereof
which comprise the legislative district.

The 1776 Constitution, with its annual legislative elections, did not contain
a provision equivalent to this paragraph. The matters of vacancies "occasioned
by death, resignation, or otherwise," and elections to fill the unexpired terms
were covered by Article IV, section 2, paragraph 2, and section 4, paragraph
1, of the 1844 Constitution. The current paragraph, with its detailed provisions
for the filling of vacancies, was adopted by amendment in 1988. This paragraph
has not been subject to significant judicial interpretation.

2. Each house shall be the judge of elections, returns and qualifications
of its own members, and a majority of all its members shall constitute a

quorum to do business; but a smaller number may adjourn from day to day, and may be authorized to compel the attendance of absent members, in such manner, and under such penalties, as each house may provide.

This paragraph's mandate that each house has the power to judge the qualifications of its own members originated in Article V of the 1776 Constitution. Article III specified the quorum of the Council, but not the Assembly. The 1844 Constitution, Article IV, section 4, paragraph 2, included a paragraph that, but for a few editorial changes, was identical to this current provision.

This provision makes the important policy choice that the *legislative branch* judges the qualifications of its own members. Therefore, the role of the courts in election contests is very restricted. The courts may, however, enforce statutes enacted by both houses that restrict external activities of legislators (Reilly v. Ozzard). The reference to "a majority of all its members" as a quorum has been interpreted by the attorney general to mean the full membership even if seats are vacant (Formal Opinion of Attorney General, No. 3 [February 6, 1961]). Furthermore, although each house has the power to "finally judicially determine" the qualifications of its members, the courts may exercise ministerial duties under statutes providing for election contests (In re Hess).

> 3. Each house shall choose its own officers, determine the rules of its proceedings, and punish its members for disorderly behavior. It may expel a member with the concurrence of two-thirds of all its members.

Article V of the 1776 Constitution empowered the assembly to choose a speaker, and Article VII required the council to choose a vice-president of the council. Article IV, section 4, paragraph 3, of the 1844 Constitution was virtually identical to this current paragraph.

This provision makes the rules of legislative procedure the province of each house. There are, however, numerous procedural limitations contained throughout Article IV which, in effect, create exceptions to this paragraph's mandate that "each house shall . . . determine the rules of its proceedings."

The constitutional power to expel a member contained in this paragraph has been held not to preclude reasonable alternative methods of expulsion provided by statute, enforceable by the courts (Reilly v. Ozzard; Errichetti v. Merlino).

> 4. Each house shall keep a journal of its proceedings, and from time to time publish the same. The yeas and nays of the members of either house on any question shall, on demand of one-fifth of those present, be entered on the journal.

This paragraph had its origin, in almost identical language, in Article IV, section 4, paragraph 4, of the 1844 Constitution. The one-fifth requirement for roll-call votes entered in the journal has been interpreted by the attorney general not to apply literally to "any question," but to be triggered only where proceedings have reached a stage where there is a question before the house. (Formal Opinion of Attorney General, No. 3 [January 5, 1950]). This paragraph has not been the subject of significant judicial interpretation.

> 5. Neither house, during the session of the Legislature, shall, without the consent of the other, adjourn for more than three days, or to any other place than that in which the two houses shall be sitting.

Article V of the 1776 Constitution permitted the Assembly to "sit upon their own adjournments." Article VI required the Council to be convened at all times when the assembly was sitting, "for which purpose the Speaker of the House of Assembly shall always, immediately after an adjournment, give notice to the Governor, or Vice-President, of the time and place to which the House is adjourned." The 1844 Constitution, Article IV, section 4, paragraph 5, was virtually identical to the current paragraph.

In a bicameral system, the unlimited power of one house to adjourn itself indefinitely would cause insurmountable problems. A provision such as this one places a three-day limit on such adjournments without the consent of the other house. Thus, a statute that was presented to the governor on the day the assembly adjourned for a period longer than the governor had to consider the bill, thereby preventing its return, was held to be unconstitutional (In re "An Act to Amend an Act Entitled 'An Act Concerning Public Utilities' ").

> 6. All bills and joint resolutions shall be read three times in each house before final passage. No bill or joint resolution shall be read a third time in either house until after the intervention of one full calendar day following the day of the second reading; but if either house shall resolve by vote of three-fourths of all its members, signified by yeas and nays entered on the journal, that a bill or joint resolution is an emergency measure, it may proceed forthwith from second to third reading. No bill or joint resolution shall pass, unless there shall be a majority of all the members of each body personally present and agreeing thereto, and the yeas and nays of the members voting on such final passage shall be entered on the journal.

This paragraph has its origins in Article III of the 1776 Constitution and Article IV, section 4, paragraph 6, of the 1844 Constitution. The requirement of a full calendar day intervening between second and third readings, except in emergencies, was added in 1947.

The provision is aimed at insuring a careful and informed deliberation on legislation, together with public awareness, and passage when a quorum is present. It requires that the vote on final passage of bills be recorded in the journal. These requirements stand as limitations on the otherwise plenary power of the legislature to enact laws.

In a 1982 decision the New Jersey Supreme Court addressed the common situation where a senate bill was received by the house and, all on the same day, read twice and substituted for an identical house bill that had been before the house for six days prior to third reading. Then, still on the same day, the senate bill was read a third time and passed. After reviewing the constitutional history of paragraph 6, the Court upheld the bill, concluding that "to satisfy the constitutional provision, then, a bill must only remain 'unchanged' before a house of the Legislature for at least one calendar day between its second and third readings . . . the Constitution does not rigidly require that any particular rite be followed in the passage of legislation." The Court observed that it was the contents of the bill that had to be before the house for at least one day (In re Application of Forsythe).

> 7. Members of the Senate and General Assembly shall receive annually, during the term for which they shall have been elected and while they shall hold their office, such compensation as shall, from time to time, be fixed by law and no other allowance or emolument, directly or indirectly, for any purpose whatever. The President of the Senate and Speaker of the General Assembly, each by virtue of his office, shall receive an additional allowance, equal to one-third of his compensation as a member.

This paragraph had its origin in Article IV, section 4, paragraph 7, of the 1844 Constitution, as amended in 1875. Those provisions set specific dollar amounts of compensation for legislators. The current provision leaves the amount of compensation up to the legislature itself to set by statute (Chamber of Commerce of Eastern Union County v. Leone). The prohibition on other forms of "allowance or emolument" has been held not to apply to pensions, which are a legitimate form of compensation (Chamber of Commerce of Eastern Union County v. Leone).

> 8. The compensation of members of the Senate and General Assembly shall be fixed at the first session of the Legislature held after this Constitution takes effect, and may be increased or decreased by law from time to time thereafter, but no increase or decrease shall be effective until the legislative year following the next general election for members of the General Assembly.

This paragraph, added by the 1947 Constitution, builds on the prior paragraph that makes legislative compensation a matter for decision by the legislature itself, but limits the implementation of any change (increase or decrease) until after the next general election for legislators. The Chancery Division has held that this paragraph's reference to "compensation" includes pensions and that the purpose of this provision is to prevent all forms of retroactive increases in compensation (Chamber of Commerce of Eastern Union County v. Leone).

> 9. Members of the Senate and General Assembly shall, in all cases except treason and high misdemeanor, be privileged from arrest during their atten-

dance at the sitting of their respective houses, and in going to and returning from the same; and for any statement, speech or debate in either house or at any meeting of a legislative committee, they shall not be questioned in any other place.

This paragraph was carried over with only minor expansions (including "statement" and legislative committee meetings) from Article IV, section 4, paragraph 8, of the 1844 Constitution. It is very similar to the federal Constitution's "speech and debate clause" and has been held to protect legislators not only from the *results* of litigation, but also from the *burden of defending* such litigation. Its protection, however, only reaches "legislative conduct . . . within a legitimate sphere of legislative activity" (State v. Gregorio). Therefore, in the Gregorio case, the court held that a legislator could be prosecuted for filing a false financial disclosure statement.

SECTION V

1. No member of the Senate or General Assembly, during the term for which he shall have been elected, shall be nominated, elected or appointed to any State civil office or position, of profit, which shall have been created by law, or the emoluments whereof shall have been increased by law, during such term. The provisions of this paragraph shall not prohibit the election of any person as Governor or as a member of the Senate or General Assembly.

This provision is basically identical to that contained in Article IV, section 5, paragraph 1, of the 1844 Constitution. Interestingly, this provision, usually referred to as the "ineligibility clause," was patterned directly after Article I, Section VI, clause 2, of the U.S. Constitution and is common in state constitutions.[30] It was apparently viewed as a necessary safeguard in 1844 when the matter of appointment of public officers was removed from legislative authority and placed in the hands of the governor. There was concern that legislators might collude with the governor and be influenced by the promise of certain appointments. The provision is a compromise between an even wider ineligibility for legislators, supported by some in the 1844 convention, and the position that there should be no ineligibility at all for legislators. The compromise renders legislators ineligible, during their terms, for offices that were created or for which the salary was increased during the legislator's term. The New Jersey Supreme Court has held that the courts do have jurisdiction to resolve disputes under this paragraph without infringing on the legislature's power to judge the qualifications of its members (Reilly v. Ozzard).

The New Jersey Supreme Court has held that a member of the legislature may not be appointed to the Supreme Court during his term of office during which the Supreme Court justices' salaries were increased (a cost-of-living increase), even though the statute increasing the salaries exempted "any present member of the Senate or General Assembly during the term for which he shall have been elected" (Vreeland v. Byrne).[31] The Court has also held, however, that a legislator is not ineligible, and therefore required to give up a civil office, when the salary increase for the office is passed during the term of the former legislator, but *after* the person assumes the office (Student Public Interest Research Group v. Byrne).

> 2. The Legislature may appoint any commission, committee or other body whose main purpose is to aid or assist it in performing its functions. Members of the Legislature may be appointed to serve on any such body.

This paragraph was added by the 1947 Constitutional Convention, and, in effect, modifies the separation of powers doctrine. It permits the legislature to create any body "whose main purpose" is legislative. Further, it permits legislators to be appointed to such body. Thus, the State Commission of Investigation, which included appointees of the legislature and governor, was upheld as a legislative commission even though it mixed the appointing authority and was directed to investigate at the request of the governor (Zicarelli v. New Jersey State Commission of Investigation).

> 3. If any member of the Legislature shall become a member of Congress or shall accept any Federal or State office or position, of profit, his seat shall thereupon become vacant.

This paragraph had its origins in Article IV, section 5, paragraph 2, of the 1844 Constitution. It implements the policy that no *state* legislator shall hold any other *federal* or *state* office or position, with the sanction of automatic forfeiture of the state legislative seat. The New Jersey Supreme Court has noted that either common law or statutory law may provide additional limitations on dual officeholding, but that neither such limitations, nor this constitutional limitation, prohibit a legislator from serving as a township attorney (Reilly v. Ozzard).

The 1844 provision spoke only of "office," and the 1947 Constitutional Convention expanded it to "office or position" apparently to overrule Wilentz ex rel. Golat v. Stanger (Reilly v. Ozzard). Stanger had held that the predecessor provision did not operate to vacate a senator's seat when he served as paid counsel to the Milk Control Board.

> 4. No member of Congress, no person holding any Federal or State office or position, of profit, and no judge of any court shall be entitled to a seat in the Legislature.

This paragraph, dating from Article IV, section 5, paragraph 3, of the 1844 Constitution, expresses the complimentary policy to that stated in the preceding paragraph. It was also expanded in 1947 to include "office or position." Its inclusion of judges dates from Article XX of the 1776 Constitution (State v. Parkhurst). The Prohibition is stated as a limitation on eligibility for state legislative seats. Persons such as commissioners of county boards of taxation may, however, run for legislative seats if they resign from the first office prior to being sworn into the legislature (Merritt v. Headley).

> 5. Neither the Legislature nor either house thereof shall elect or appoint any executive, administrative or judicial officer except the State Auditor.

This paragraph, added by the 1947 Constitutional Convention, eliminated the last vestiges of the system of legislative appointment of officials in the executive and judicial branches. It implemented the general separation of powers philosophy of the 1947 Constitution. The exception for the state auditor, who examines the expenditure of state funds, recognizes that this office is essentially a legislative office. The State Commission of Investigation, to which the legislature and governor each appointed two members, was upheld as a legislative function (Zicarelli v. New Jersey State Commission of Investigation). The legislature may, by law, provide for the appointment, by proper constitutional authority, such as the governor (Richman v. Ligham).

SECTION VI

> 1. All bills for raising revenue shall originate in the General Assembly; but the Senate may propose or concur with amendments, as on other bills.

This paragraph originated in Article VI of the 1776 Constitution, which provided that "the Council [upper house] . . . shall not prepare or alter any money bill—which shall be the privilege of the Assembly." This reflected the prevailing view during the Revolution that revenue bills should only originate in the "popular" branch of the legislature, as was the practice in England (Township of Bernards v. Allen). New Jersey's provision was particularly strict, however, in prohibiting the Council from even altering a money bill. Article IV, section 6, paragraph 1, of the 1844 Constitution eased this restriction, by stating "but the Senate may propose or concur with amendments, as on other bills," after an attempt to remove the provision entirely was unsuccessful. This current paragraph is virtually identical, having survived an attempt to remove it in the 1947 Constitutional Convention.

The Supreme Court has held that the "bill origin clause" does not apply to a bill raising revenue by the sale of bonds for a specific project, which is approved by the electorate pursuant to Article VIII, Section II, paragraph 3 (Kervick v. Bontempo). The Court does not take an expansive view of the term "bills for raising revenue" (State v. Thermoid Co.), but there are examples of legislation being declared invalid for violating the bill origin clause (Thiokol Chemical Corp. v. Morris Co. Bd. of Taxation).

2. The Legislature may enact general laws under which municipalities, other than counties, may adopt zoning ordinances limiting and restricting to specified districts and regulating therein, buildings and structures, according to their construction, and the nature and extent of their use, and the nature and extent of the uses of land, and the exercise of such authority shall be deemed to be within the police power of the State. Such laws shall be subject to repeal or alteration by the Legislature.

This paragraph was added to the Constitution by an amendment adopted in 1927. The amendment was necessary to "overrule" a 1923 decision of the Supreme Court holding that the legislative authorization to localities to enact zoning ordinances was an unconstitutional attempt to use the police power to interfere with private property rights (Ignaciunas v. Risley).[32] The 1927 amendment appeared as Article IV, section 6, paragraph 5, of the 1844 Constitution. An attempt to authorize the legislature to permit *counties* to exercise the zoning power, by eliminating "other than counties," was defeated in 1947.[33]

In 1956 in Roselle v. Wright the New Jersey Supreme Court stated that the 1927 amendment did not grant any *new* power to the legislature beyond the basic police power, which is the source of the power to zone. The Court continued:

The police power does not have its genesis in a written constitution. It is an essential element of the social compact, an attribute of sovereignty itself, possessed by the states before the adoption of the Federal Constitution.

These constitutional provisions relating to zoning were designed to remedy the judicial denials of the fullness of the power and to regulate its use so as to accommodate essential common and individual rights in the fulfillment of the principle.

In the well-known Mt. Laurel decisions, the New Jersey Supreme Court held that the zoning power, as part of the police power that permits the government to regulate to protect health, safety, and welfare, must always be used to further the general welfare. The Court struck down the exclusion, by zoning, of low- and moderate-income housing by local governments (Southern Burlington County NAACP v. Township of Mt. Laurel; Hills Development Co. v. Bernards Township).[34] The courts will review zoning ordinances to make sure they are reasonable (Borough of Glassboro v. Vallorosi).

3. Any agency or political subdivision of the State or any agency of a political subdivision thereof, which may be empowered to take or otherwise acquire private property for any public highway, parkway, airport, place, improvement, or use, may be authorized by law to take or otherwise acquire a fee simple absolute or any lesser interest, and may be authorized by law to take or otherwise acquire a fee simple absolute in, easements upon, or the benefit of restrictions upon, abutting property to preserve and protect the public highway, parkway, airport, place, improvement, or use; but such taking shall be with just compensation.

This paragraph has its origins in the 1844 Constitution in Article I, section 16, and Article IV, section 7, paragraph 9 (renumbered paragraph 8 by an 1875 amendment). The current paragraph must be read together with Article I, paragraph 20, of the current constitution. See discussion under that paragraph.

This paragraph, which is concerned only with takings of property (condemnation, or, the power of eminent domain) by the government, was made much more specific by the 1947 Constitution. It clearly authorizes the taking of an interest in land that is less than fee simple (complete title); the taking of an interest in land which abuts that which has been taken for a public use (referred to as excess condemnation). The New Jersey Supreme Court has recognized that the power of eminent domain is inherent in the legislative branch and that therefore the state constitutional provisions do not grant this power, but merely operate to limit it (Abbott v. Beth Israel Cemetery Association). This paragraph also clearly recognizes that the legislature may delegate its power of eminent domain to state agencies and local governments, and its specific listing of illustrative purposes for takings constitutes a presumptive recognition that those purposes are public uses (Aviation Services, Inc. v. Board of Adjustment of Hanover Township).

As indicated earlier, in the discussion of Article I, paragraph 20, the power of eminent domain is subject to complex statutory procedures, and the notions of "taking," "use," and "just compensation" have been the source of much litigation.[35]

> 4. The Legislature, in order to insure continuity of State, county and local governmental operations in periods of emergency resulting from disasters caused by enemy attack, shall have the power and the immediate and continuing duty by legislation (1) to provide, prior to the occurrence of the emergency, for prompt and temporary succession to the powers and duties of public offices, of whatever nature and whether filled by election or appointment, the incumbents of which may become unavailable for carrying on the powers and duties of such offices, and (2) to adopt such other measures as may be necessary and proper for insuring the continuity of governmental operations. In the exercise of the powers hereby conferred the Legislature shall in all respects conform to the requirements of this Constitution except to the extent that in the judgment of the Legislature to do so would be impracticable or would admit of undue delay.

This paragraph had no predecessor in the earlier constitutions. It was added by amendment in 1961 to provide mechanisms for continuing governmental operation "in periods of emergency resulting from disasters caused by enemy attack" and reflects, in important respects, the concerns of the 1950s and 1960s about nuclear attack. It specifies the legislature as the branch to formulate plans ahead of time to deal with such a disaster and permits, under the prescribed circumstances, the legislature to act without following the constitution. The legislature has implemented the provision through various statutes in Title 52 of the New Jersey Statutes Annotated.

This paragraph has not been the subject of judicial interpretation.

SECTION VII

1. No divorce shall be granted by the Legislature.

This provision was added as Article IV, section 7, paragraph 1, in the 1844 Constitution. It ensures that divorce is dealt with by general laws that apply the same rules to everyone rather than on a case-by-case basis by the legislature. A major criticism had been the amount of time the legislature spent on individual divorce bills and the extent to which these bills interfered with, and influenced, other legislative matters. The provision has not been the subject of significant judicial interpretation.

2. No gambling of any kind shall be authorized by the Legislature unless the specific kind, restrictions and control thereof have been heretofore submitted to, and authorized by a majority of the votes cast by, the people at a special election or shall hereafter be submitted to, and authorized by a majority of the votes cast thereon by, the legally qualified voters of the State voting at a general election, except that, without any such submission or authorization:

A. It shall be lawful for bona fide veterans, charitable, educational, religious or fraternal organizations, civic and service clubs, senior citizen associations or clubs, volunteer fire companies and first-aid or rescue squads to conduct, under such restrictions and control as shall from time to time be prescribed by the Legislature by law, games of chance of, and restricted to, the selling of rights to participate, the awarding of prizes, in the specific kind of game of chance sometimes known as bingo or lotto, played with cards bearing numbers or other designations, 5 or more in one line, the holder covering numbers as objects, similarly numbered, are drawn from a receptacle and the game being won by the person who first covers a previously designated arrangement of numbers on such a card, when the entire net proceeds of such games of chance are to be devoted to educational, charitable, patriotic, religious or public-spirited uses, and in the case of senior citizen associations or clubs to the support of such organizations, in any municipality, in which a majority of the qualified voters, voting thereon, at a general or special election as the submission thereof shall be prescribed by the Legislature by law, shall authorize the conduct of such games of chance therein;

B. It shall be lawful for the Legislature to authorize, by law, bona fide veterans, charitable, educational, religious or fraternal organizations, civic and service clubs, senior citizen associations or clubs, volunteer fire companies and first-aid or rescue squads to conduct games of chance of, and restricted to, the selling of rights to participate, and the awarding of prizes, in the specific kinds of games of chance sometimes known as raffles, conducted by the drawing for prizes or by the allotment of prizes by chance, when the entire net proceeds of such games of chance are to be devoted to educational, charitable, patriotic, religious or public-spirited uses, and in the case of senior citizen associations or clubs to the support of such organizations, in any municipality, in which such law shall be adopted by a majority of the qualified voters, voting thereon, at a general or special election as the submission thereof shall be prescribed by law and for the Legislature, from time to time, to restrict and control, by law, the conduct of such games of chance;

C. It shall be lawful for the Legislature to authorize the conduct of State lotteries restricted to the selling of rights to participate therein and the awarding of prizes by drawings when the entire net proceeds of any such lottery shall be for State institutions, State aid for education; and

D. It shall be lawful for the Legislature to authorize by law the establishment and operation, under regulation and control by the State, of gambling houses or casinos within the boundaries, as heretofore established, of the city of Atlantic City, county of Atlantic, and to license and tax such operations and equipment used in connection therewith. Any law authorizing the establishment and operation of such gambling establishments shall provide for the State revenues derived therefrom to be applied solely for the purpose of providing funding for reductions in property taxes, rental, telephone, gas, electric, and municipal utilities charges of, eligible senior citizens and disabled residents of the State, and for additional or expanded health services or benefits or transportation services or benefits to eligible senior citizens and disabled residents, in accordance with such formulae as the Legislature shall by law provide. The type and number of such casinos or gambling houses and of the gambling games which may be conducted in any such establishment shall be determined by or pursuant to the terms of the law authorizing the establishment and operation thereof.

This provision is probably the single most-often amended section of the New Jersey Constitution. Originally inserted in 1844 as an anti-lottery limit on the legislature, it was amended in 1897 to ban the legislature from authorizing all forms of gambling. This set the stage for the various exceptions to the ban that have been adopted through the years, which were a major focus of the 1947 Constitutional Convention, and are reflected in the current version of the provision. The evolution of these provisions is traced in Carll & Ramagosa, Inc. v. Ash. The current provisions give the electorate an ongoing role in approving various forms of gambling, both through the operation of the introductory section and through the process of approving exceptions such as those contained in subparagraphs A through D. In 1985 the Supreme Court reviewed the operation of this entire provision on gambling, and invalidated a statute providing for intertrack betting on simulcast horse racing because this "specific kind" of gambling had not been approved by the voters as required by this paragraph (Atlantic City Racing Association v. Attorney General).

Judicial interpretation of these provisions has aimed at applying the constitutional terms such as "lotteries," "bingo," and so forth.

> 3. The Legislature shall not pass any bill of attainder, ex post facto law,
> or law impairing the obligation of contracts, or depriving a party of any
> remedy for enforcing a contract which existed when the contract was made.

This paragraph, virtually unchanged from 1844, contains a number of related limits on the legislature concerning retroactive laws. A bill of attainder is a statute in which the legislature determines the guilt of named or readily ascertainable individuals without the opportunity for a judicial trial (Matter of Coruzzi). The prohibition on ex post facto laws applies, generally, only to criminal laws that make conduct criminal or increase penalties for criminal acts after such acts have been committed. Therefore, many civil penalties, even if applied retroactively, do not violate the ex post facto clause (Matter of Garay). The New Jersey Supreme Court has held that ex post facto principles not only limit the legislature, but also restrict retroactive judicial interpretations of criminal laws (State v. Young).

With respect to contracts, the paragraph not only prohibits laws "impairing the obligation for contracts," as does the federal Constitution, but goes on to bar the deprivation of contract remedies in existence at the time the contract was made. Each of these types of laws are also, by their nature, "retroactive." Not all laws that affect contract rights already in existence, however, are invalid as an unconstitutional impairment of the obligation of contract. The New Jersey Supreme Court stated in South Hamilton Associates v. Mayor and Council of the Town of Morristown:

It is well-established that legislation that has as its rational public purpose the necessary protection of the health, safety, and welfare of the public, and is within the police power of the state or its subdivisions, may be applied retroactively to alter or abrogate existing contractual rights without affecting its validity under the contract clause of the United States or New Jersey Constitutions.

In South Hamilton the court struck down the statute, but it indicated clearly that contract rights are subject to police power regulations. It is often the holders of government bonds who claim impairment of their contract rights (statutory and contractual mechanisms to pay off the bonds) when statutes modify those rights (Fidelity Union Trust Co. v. New Jersey Highway Authority). Public officers do not have contract rights to the receipt of compensation (Matter of Coruzzi).

The prohibition on depriving parties to contracts of remedies existing when the contract was made has been held not to prohibit laws altering the procedural methods of enforcing contracts as long as the value of the contract right is not substantially reduced (Lapp v. Belvedere).

4. To avoid improper influences which may result from intermixing in one and the same act such things as have no proper relation to each other, every law shall embrace but one object, and that shall be expressed in the title. This paragraph shall not invalidate any law adopting or enacting a compilation, consolidation, revision or rearrangement of all or parts of the statutory law.

This paragraph dates from the 1844 Constitution, with the last sentence permitting general statutory compilations or revisions being added in 1875. However, the 1702 Instructions from Queen Anne to Lord Cornbury in New Jersey, paragraph 18, contained the following similar directive:

You are also as much as possible to observe in the passing of all laws, that whatever may be requisite upon each different matter be accordingly provided for by a different law without intermixing in one and the same Act, such things as have no proper relation to each other; and you are especially to take care that no clause or clauses be inserted in, or annexed to any Act which shall be foreign to what the Title of such respective Act imports.[36]

The provision contains two separate, but related limits on legislative lawmaking procedure:[37] (1) each law can only concern one "object," and (2) the title of the law must disclose that object. Although alleged violations of this provision are often raised in litigation, they are rarely successful. The single object requirement seeks to prevent "logrolling," whereby unrelated statutory provisions that would not command majority votes in the legislature are lumped together in one bill in the hopes that a coalition of minorities will come together to provide a majority vote. It also seeks to require separate deliberation on unrelated measures (New Jersey Association on Correction v. Lan).

The title requirement is a disclosure device, requiring a title that gives general notice of the contents of the bill (State v. Zelinski).

Article VIII, Section II, paragraph 3 is another, more specific, single-object rule for statutes creating state debt.

5. No law shall be revived or amended by reference to its title only, but the act revived, or the section or sections amended, shall be inserted at length. No act shall be passed which shall provide that any existing law, or any part thereof, shall be made or deemed a part of the act or which shall enact that any existing law, or any part thereof, shall be applicable, except by inserting it in such act.

This provision was added by amendment in 1875 to Article IV, section 7, paragraph 4, of the 1844 Constitution. It also included the prohibition on special laws now found in paragraph 7. The 1947 Constitution established this as a separate paragraph 5.

This paragraph is aimed at disclosure in the lawmaking process. It prohibits revival (reenactment of a law that has been repealed) or amendment of laws by referring only to the title of such laws. It requires, rather, that the text of the law that is revived or amended be included in the bill so the reader can see, on the face of the bill, the legal changes that are proposed. The paragraph also, based on the same philosophy, prohibits "adoption by reference" of existing laws.

The second limitation has not been interpreted literally by the courts. In the words of the Appellate Division in Township of Princeton v. Bardin:

> The purpose of this provision in our State Constitution is for the "suppression of deceptive and fraudulent legislation, the purpose and meaning of which [can] not be discovered either by the legislature or the public without an examination of and a comparison with other statutes." . . . The provision is not meant to "obstruct or embarrass legislation," but rather "to secure a fair and intelligent exercise of the lawmaking power." . . . Because it limits legislative power, the courts have strictly construed the section.

The court in Princeton held that a tax exemption statute that referred to a section of the *federal* Internal Revenue Code did not violate this limitation, concluding that it was "an efficient and practical method of defining the kinds of nonprofit organizations contemplated by the Legislature for eligibility under the act." The Supreme Court has stated that if an act "properly embodies complete legislation in itself it may refer to auxiliary laws on the subject without violating the constitutional provision" (Eggers v. Kenny; Suburban Savings and Loan Association v. Commissioner of Banking).

> 6. The laws of this State shall begin in the following style: "Be it enacted by the Senate and General Assembly of the State of New Jersey."

This paragraph has its origins in Article XV of the 1776 Constitution, and Article IV, section 7, paragraph 5, of the 1844 Constitution. It is intended to signal an exercise of the formal lawmaking power, rather than a less important expression of legislative action such as a resolution. It has not been the subject of important judicial interpretation.

> 7. No general law shall embrace any provision of a private, special or local character.

This paragraph was carried over verbatim from the 1875 amendment inserting this sentence into Article IV, section 7, paragraph 4, of the 1844 Constitution. The 1870s was a decade of widespread concern about state legislatures, particularly the subject of special laws.[38] It must be considered together with the following two paragraphs.

The Supreme Court has noted that the "vice in special laws is that they foster favoritism. The purpose of the constitutional prohibitions is to prevent abuse of the legislative process by picking favorites'' (Jordan v. Horseman's Benevolent and Protective Assoc.). The Court referred to the following test:

The essence of unconstitutional special legislation is the arbitrary exclusion of someone from the class. In considering whether legislation is general or special, the Court must make three determinations: (1) the purpose and subject matter of the statute; (2) whether any persons are excluded who should be included; and (3) whether the classification is reasonable, given the purpose of the statute.

(See also Newark Superior Officers Association v. City of Newark.)

> 8. No private, special or local law shall be passed unless public notice of the intention to apply therefor, and of the general object thereof, shall have been previously given. Such notice shall be given at such time and in such manner and shall be so evidenced and the evidence thereof shall be so preserved as may be provided by law.

This paragraph, added by amendment in 1875, applies to those areas where, under paragraphs 7 and 9, private, special, or local laws may be passed by the legislature. It institutes the interesting requirement of public notice prior to the enactment of such a law. Therefore, even if an act is held not to be an unconstitutional special law, it may be invalidated for failure to comply with this notice requirement (Meadowlands Regional Development Agency v. State).

The mechanisms for notice required by this paragraph are contained in N.J.S.A. § 1:6–1 et seq.

> 9. The Legislature shall not pass any private, special or local laws:
>
> (1) Authorizing the sale of any lands belonging in whole or in part to a minor or minors or other persons who may at the time be under any legal disability to act for themselves.
>
> (2) Changing the law of descent.
>
> (3) Providing for change of venue in civil or criminal causes.
>
> (4) Selecting, drawing, summoning or empaneling grand or petit jurors.
>
> (5) Creating, increasing or decreasing the emoluments, term or tenure rights of any public officers or employees.
>
> (6) Relating to taxation or exemption therefrom.
>
> (7) Providing for the management and control of free public schools.
>
> (8) Granting to any corporation, association or individual any exclusive privilege, immunity or franchise whatever.
>
> (9) Granting to any corporation, association or individual the right to lay down railroad tracks.
>
> (10) Laying out, opening, altering, constructing, maintaining and repairing roads or highways.

(11) Vacating any road, town plot, street, alley or public grounds.

(12) Appointing local officers or commissions to regulate municipal affairs.

(13) Regulating the internal affairs of municipalities formed for local government and counties, except as otherwise in this Constitution provided.

The Legislature shall pass general laws providing for the cases enumerated in this paragraph, and for all other cases which, in its judgment, may be provided for by general laws. The Legislature shall pass no special act conferring corporate powers, but shall pass general laws under which corporations may be organized and corporate powers of every nature obtained, subject, nevertheless, to repeal or alteration at the will of the Legislature.

This paragraph, also adopted by amendment in 1875, builds upon the general prohibitions of the preceding two paragraphs by incorporating in the constitution a specific list of subject areas on which the legislature may not legislate by private, special, or local law. The paragraph goes on to mandate, rather, that the legislature pass general laws in these areas and make specific prohibition, in addition to (8), of special laws granting corporate powers, which had been the subject of much of the abuse in the use of special laws. Finally, the paragraph makes clear that general corporate statutes, under which corporations are formed and operate, may be altered or repealed by the legislature. This is to avoid the argument that a corporation, which has organized itself in reliance on a particular corporate statute, has a "contract" right that may not be "impaired" by the legislature (see Article IV, Section VII, paragraph 3).

The list of specific subject areas contained in the 1875 amendment was modified and reorganized by the 1947 Constitutional Convention, and numbers (1) and (6) were added.

Very soon after the adoption of the 1875 amendments, the argument was made that the question of whether a specific subject was susceptible to special legislation, or, on the other hand, was more properly the subject of general legislation was a matter for the legislature to decide without judicial interference. Justice Bennet Van Syckle of the Supreme Court firmly rejected this assertion in 1878 (Pell v. Newark).

This paragraph has generated a tremendous amount of litigation over questions as to whether a law is special, and if so, whether it falls into one of the prohibited classes.

10. Upon petition by the governing body of any municipal corporation formed for local government, or of any county, and by vote of two-thirds of all the members of each house, the Legislature may pass private, special or local laws regulating the internal affairs of the municipality or county. The petition shall be authorized in a manner to be prescribed by general law and shall specify the general nature of the law sought to be passed. Such

law shall become operative only if it is adopted by ordinance of the governing body of the municipality or county or by vote of the legally qualified voters thereof. The Legislature shall prescribe in such law or by general law the method of adopting such law, and the manner in which the ordinance of adoption may be enacted or the vote taken, as the case may be.

This paragraph was added by the 1947 Constitutional Convention. It creates an express constitutional exception to the prohibitions of paragraph 9 (13), by permitting the legislature, by a two-thirds vote, to pass special laws concerning municipalities and counties when, by petition from the governing body of the city or county, it is requested to pass such special laws. Thus, if there is a situation that must be dealt with by special law, in the opinion of the local government, the limitation on special legislation is lifted as provided in this paragraph.

The statutory mechanisms for petitioning the Legislature under this paragraph are contained in N.J.S.A. § 1:6–10 et seq.

11. The provisions of this Constitution and of any law concerning municipal corporations formed for local government, or concerning counties, shall be liberally construed in their favor. The powers of counties and such municipal corporations shall include not only those granted in express terms but also those of necessary or fair implication, or incident to the powers expressly conferred, or essential thereto, and not inconsistent with or prohibited by this Constitution or by law.

This is a rule of constitutional interpretation, placed within the text of the constitution itself. It is intended to reverse the outmoded view that the powers of local governments should be strictly construed, or, in effect, disfavored. It works essentially to resolve doubts about local government powers in favor of their existence (Inganamort v. Borough of Fort Lee).

SECTION VIII

1. Members of the Legislature shall, before they enter on the duties of their respective offices, take and subscribe the following oath or affirmation: "I do solemnly swear (or affirm) that I will support the Constitution of the United States and the Constitution of the State of New Jersey, and that I will faithfully discharge the duties of Senator (or member of the General Assembly) according to the best of my ability." Members-elect of the Senate or General Assembly are empowered to administer said oath or affirmation to each other.

This paragraph, requiring legislators to take an oath or affirmation of office, has its origin in Article XXIII of the 1776 Constitution, under which legislators had to swear not to vote for laws injurious to the public welfare, or interfering with voting, jury trial, or religious rights. This current version was carried over without substantial change from Article IV, section 8, of the 1844 Constitution.

When, in 1949, the legislature sought to add, by statute, to the oath of office for legislators the requirement that they swear that they did not believe in the use of force or unconstitutional means to overthrow the government, and disavow membership in organizations having such beliefs, the New Jersey Supreme Court struck the statute down. It held that the constitutionally mandated oath was exclusive and could not be supplemented by the legislature (Imbrie v. Marsh). The Imbrie decision contains an exhaustive treatment of the constitutional and statutory history of oaths in New Jersey.

> 2. Every officer of the Legislature shall, before he enters upon his duties, take and subscribe the following oath or affirmation: "I do solemnly promise and swear (or affirm) that I will faithfully, impartially and justly perform all the duties of the office of _____, to the best of my ability and understanding; that I will carefully preserve all records, papers, writings, or property entrusted to me for safekeeping by virtue of my office, and make such disposition of the same as may be required by law."

This paragraph, added in 1947, provides a specific additional oath for *officers* of the legislature. It has not been the subject of judicial interpretation.

Article V

Executive

SECTION I

1. The executive power shall be vested in a Governor.

This apparently simple statement, with its origins in Article VIII of the 1776 Constitution and carried over verbatim from Article V, section 1, of the 1844 Constitution, sets forth the assignment of "executive" power to the governor.

A prime objective of the 1947 Constitutional Convention was to create a strong executive.[39] Referring to the governor's power to investigate and remove state officers and employees, the New Jersey Supreme Court noted in Russo v. Meyner:

Our constitutional history shows us that the authority granted to the Governor was but one of the steps on the long road back from the post-Revolutionary reaction to the attitudes of colonial governors which led the framers of our earliest Constitution to look with suspicion upon the grant of any great power to the Governor.

This paragraph is often referred to, together with a specific grant of executive power elsewhere in Article V, as the basis for implied powers of the governor.

2. The Governor shall not be less than thirty years of age, and shall have been for at least twenty years a citizen of the United States, and a resident of this State seven years next before his election, unless he shall have been absent during that time on the public business of the United States or of this State.

This paragraph, carried over from Article V, section 4, of the 1844 Constitution with only minor editorial changes, sets forth the basic eligibility requirements for the office of governor. It has not been subject to judicial interpretation.

> 3. No member of Congress or person holding any office or position, of profit, under this State or the United States shall be Governor. If the Governor or person administering the office of Governor shall accept any other office or position, of profit, under this State or the United States, his office of Governor shall thereby be vacated. No Governor shall be elected by the Legislature to any office during the term for which he shall have been elected Governor.

This paragraph, similar to Article IV, Section V, paragraph 4, for legislators, prohibits the governor from serving in any other state or federal office and includes the automatic sanction of the office being deemed vacated in the event of a violation. This paragraph is based on Article V, section 8, of the 1844 Constitution, with the last sentence added in 1875 and modified by the 1947 Constitution further to effectuate separation of powers doctrine.

The paragraph has not been subject to judicial review and has been referred to by the New Jersey Supreme Court as one which is straightforward in nature and requires little in the way of judicial construction (Vreeland v. Byrne).

> 4. The Governor shall be elected by the legally qualified voters of this State. The person receiving the greatest number of votes shall be the Governor; but if two or more shall be equal and greatest in votes, one of them shall be elected Governor by the vote of a majority of all the members of both houses in joint meeting at the regular legislative session next following the election for Governor by the people. Contested elections for the office of Governor shall be determined in such manner as may be provided by law.

This paragraph has its origins in Article V, section 2, of the 1844 Constitution. Article II, paragraph 1, of the current constitution requires the election of the governor and members of the legislature at general elections. Therefore, a similar requirement in this provision in the 1844 Constitution was deleted in the 1947 constitution. This paragraph has not been subject to judicial interpretation.

> 5. The term of office of the Governor shall be four years, beginning at noon of the third Tuesday in January next following his election, and ending at noon of the third Tuesday in January four years thereafter. No person who has been elected Governor for two successive terms, including an unexpired term, shall again be eligible for that office until the third Tuesday in January of the fourth year following the expiration of his second successive term.

This paragraph is based on Article V, section 3, of the 1844 Constitution. The 1947 revision expanded the term of office from three to four years and permitted a governor to succeed himself. It did institute the two-term limit, with the possibility of succession after an intervening term. This provision has not been subject to judicial interpretation.

6. In the event of a vacancy in the office of Governor resulting from the death, resignation or removal of a Governor in office, or the death of a Governor-elect, or from any other cause, the functions, powers, duties and emoluments of the office shall devolve upon the President of the Senate, for the time being, and in the event of his death, resignation or removal, then upon the Speaker of the General Assembly, for the time being; and in the event of his death, resignation or removal, then upon such officers and in such order of succession as may be provided by law; until a new Governor shall be elected and qualify.

This paragraph is based on Article V, sections 12 (as amended in 1897), 13, and 14 of the 1844 Constitution, which provided the same succession in office. The legislature has provided for further succession, as required by this paragraph, in N.J.S.A. § 52:14A–4.

If, pursuant to this paragraph, the "functions, powers, duties and emoluments of the office [of governor] shall devolve" on the enumerated officers they are not actually considered governor (Clifford v. Heller), but just as exercising gubernatorial powers on an interim basis and may continue to perform their other duties, such as president of the senate (Ackerman Dairy, Inc. v. Kandle).

7. In the event of the failure of the Governor-elect to qualify, or of the absence from the State of a Governor in office, or his inability to discharge the duties of his office, or his impeachment, the functions, powers, duties and emoluments of the office shall devolve upon the President of the Senate, for the time being; and in the event of his death, resignation, removal, absence, inability or impeachment, then upon the Speaker of the General Assembly, for the time being; and in the event of his death, resignation, removal, absence, inability or impeachment, then upon such officers and in such order of succession as may be provided by law; until the Governor-elect shall qualify, or the Governor in office shall return to the State, or shall no longer be unable to discharge the duties of the office, or shall be acquitted, as the case may be, or until a new Governor shall be elected and qualify.

This paragraph is based on Article V, sections 12 (as amended in 1897), 13, and 14 of the 1844 Constitution, which provided the same succession in office. This provision sets forth a succession mechanism in case a person elected governor does not qualify for office (Article V, Section I, paragraph 2) or under other temporary or permanent circumstances. The courts have treated this paragraph like they have treated paragraph 6, and it has been similarly implemented by the legislature.

8. Whenever a Governor-elect shall have failed to qualify within six months after the beginning of his term of office, or whenever for a period of six months a Governor in office, or person administering the office, shall have remained continuously absent from the State, or shall have been continuously unable to discharge the duties of his office by reason of mental or

physical disability, the office shall be deemed vacant. Such vacancy shall be determined by the Supreme Court upon presentment to it of a concurrent resolution declaring the ground of the vacancy, adopted by a vote of two-thirds of all the members of each house of the Legislature, and upon notice, hearing before the Court and proof of the existence of the vacancy.

This paragraph did not have an equivalent in the 1844 Constitution. It puts a six-month limit on the circumstances that would permit another officer, such as the president of the senate, to exercise the powers of governor. It sets up a procedure for declaring a vacancy in office, after which an election for a new governor can be conducted pursuant to paragraph 9. This provision has not been the subject of judicial interpretation.

9. In the event of a vacancy in the office of Governor, a Governor shall be elected to fill the unexpired term at the general election next succeeding the vacancy, unless the vacancy shall occur within sixty days immediately preceding a general election, in which case he shall be elected at the second succeeding general election; but no election to fill an unexpired term shall be held in any year in which a Governor is to be elected for a full term. A Governor elected for an unexpired term shall assume his office immediately upon his election.

This paragraph, also new in 1947, creates the mechanism for electing a governor to fill an unexpired term created by a vacancy in office. It has not been the subject of judicial interpretation.

10. The Governor shall receive for his services a salary, which shall be neither increased nor diminished during the period for which he shall have been elected.

This paragraph is based on Article V, section 5, of the 1844 Constitution. It protects the governor from a reduction in his salary and prohibits an increase during his term of office. It has not been the subject of significant judicial interpretation.

11. The Governor shall take care that the laws be faithfully executed. To this end he shall have power, by appropriate action or proceeding in the courts brought in the name of the State, to enforce compliance with any constitutional or legislative mandate, or to restrain violation of any constitutional or legislative power or duty, by any officer, department or agency of the State; but this power shall not be construed to authorize any action or proceeding against the Legislature.

This paragraph begins the enumeration of specific gubernatorial powers, elaborating the assignment of the executive power to the governor in paragraph 1. Article V, section 6, of the 1844 Constitution contained the power and duty to execute the laws faithfully. The rest of the paragraph was new in 1947 and was held to permit the governor to go to court to invalidate a contract that violated public policy (Driscoll v. Burlington-Bristol Bridge Co.).

The duty to "take care that the laws be faithfully executed" carries with it a range of necessary implied gubernatorial powers, often exercised through the use of executive orders. Sometimes these powers are referred to by the courts as "inherent" powers (Kenny v. Byrne). In the Kenny case, the Appellate Division stated "unmistakably, the executive power reposed in the Governor under the Constitution, expressed in terse comprehensive terms, must be given life and meaning by investing him with the authority to implement his responsibilities. . . . To conclude otherwise is to negate the intent of the framers of the Constitution of 1947."

The power of the governor to issue executive orders, however, is limited by the requirement that it be supported by some statutory or constitutional authority, which the executive order implements (Association of New Jersey State College Faculties, Inc. v. Board of Higher Education; Worthington v. Fauver). Significant questions have arisen concerning the New Jersey governors' use of executive orders in the areas of environmental protection and preservation, such as with respect to the Pinelands and coastal development, but these controversies were resolved through the political process without definitive judicial pronouncements. (New Jersey Builders Association vs. Byrne)

> 12. The Governor shall communicate to the Legislature, by message at the opening of each regular session and at such other times as he may deem necessary, the condition of the State, and shall in like manner recommend such measures as he may deem desirable. He may convene the Legislature, or the Senate alone, whenever in his opinion the public interest shall require. He shall be the Commander-in-Chief of all the military and naval forces of the State. He shall grant commissions to all officers elected or appointed pursuant to this Constitution. He shall nominate and appoint, with the advice and consent of the Senate, all officers for whose election or appointment provision is not otherwise made by this Constitution or by law.

This paragraph continues the enumeration of powers and duties of the governor. It has its origins in Articles VI and VIII of the 1776 Constitution, and Article V, section 6, and Article VII, section 2, paragraph 9, of the 1844 Constitution. The governor's annual message to the legislature has been an important tool for executive leadership. The governor's power to convene the legislature or the senate alone (added in 1875) must be read together with Article IV, Section I, paragraph 4, which authorizes the governor to call special sessions of the legislature. The governor's residual appointment power, for those officers whose manner of selection is not otherwise provided for, eliminates the last vestiges of appointment of officials by the legislature.

The practice of senatorial courtesy, whereby gubernatorial nominations will not be made unless cleared by the senator from whose district the nominee comes, has acted as a significant limitation on the governor's appointment power although it is not provided for anywhere in the constitution.[40] This provision has not been the subject of significant judicial interpretation.

> 13. The Governor may fill any vacancy occurring in any office during a recess of the Legislature, appointment to which may be made by the Governor with the advice and consent of the Senate, or by the Legislature in joint meeting. An ad interim appointment so made shall expire at the end of the next regular session of the Senate, unless a successor shall be sooner appointed and qualify; and after the end of the session no ad interim appointment to the same office shall be made unless the Governor shall have submitted to the Senate a nomination to the office during the session and the Senate shall have adjourned without confirming or rejecting it. No person nominated for any office shall be eligible for an ad interim appointment to such office if the nomination shall have failed of confirmation by the Senate.

This paragraph, continuing the enumeration of gubernatorial powers and duties, specifies in detail the process of making temporary appointments (ad interim) while the legislature is not in session. It has its origins in Article V, section 12, of the 1844 Constitution. The provision is written to place significant limits on the interim appointment power of the governor, to avoid his abuse of the senate's power of ''advice and consent'' over appointments.

> 14. (a) When a bill has finally passed both houses, the house in which final action was taken to complete its passage shall cause it to be presented to the Governor before the close of the calendar day next following the date of the session at which such final action was taken.
>
> (b) A passed bill presented to the Governor shall become law:
>
> (1) if the Governor approves and signs it within the period allowed for his consideration; or,
>
> (2) if the Governor does not return it to the house of origin, with a statement of his objections, before the expiration of the period allowed for his consideration; or,
>
> (3) if, upon reconsideration of a bill objected to by the Governor, two-thirds of all the members of each house agree to pass the bill.
>
> (c) The period allowed for the Governor's consideration of a passed bill shall be from the date of presentation until noon of the forty-fifth day next following or, if the house of origin be in temporary adjournment on that day, the first day subsequent upon which the house reconvenes; except that:
>
> (1) if on the said forty-fifth day the Legislature is in adjournment sine die, any bill then pending the Governor's approval shall be returned, if he

objects to it, at a special session held pursuant to subparagraph (d) of this paragraph;

(2) any bill passed between the forty-fifth day and the tenth day preceding the expiration of the second legislative year shall be returned by the Governor, if he objects to it, not later than noon of the day next preceding the expiration of the second legislative year;

(3) any bill passed within 10 days preceding the expiration of the second legislative year shall become law only if the Governor signs it prior to noon of the seventh day following such expiration, or the Governor returns it to the House of origin, with a statement of his objections, and two-thirds of all members of each House agree to pass the bill prior to such expiration.

(d) For the purpose of permitting the return of bills pursuant to this paragraph, a special session of the Legislature shall convene, without petition or call, for the sole purpose of acting upon bills returned by the Governor, on the forty-fifth day next following adjournment sine die of the regular session; or, if the second legislative year of a 2–year Legislature will expire before said forty-fifth day, then the day next preceding the expiration of the legislative year.

(e) Upon receiving from the Governor a bill returned by him with his objections, the house in which it originated shall enter the objections at large in its journal or minutes and proceed to reconsider it. If, upon reconsideration, on or after the third day following its return, or the first day of a special session convened for the sole purpose of acting on such bills, two-thirds of all the members of the house of origin agree to pass the bill, it shall be sent, together with the objections of the Governor, to the other house; and if, upon reconsideration, it is approved by two-thirds of all the members of the house, it shall become a law. In all such cases the votes of each house shall be determined by yeas and nays, and the names of the persons voting for and against the bill shall be entered on the journal or minutes of each house.

(f) The Governor, in returning with his objections a bill for reconsideration at any general or special session of the Legislature, may recommend that an amendment or amendments specified by him be made in the bill, and in such case the Legislature may amend and reenact the bill. If a bill be so amended and reenacted, it shall be presented again to the Governor, but shall become a law only if he shall sign it within 10 days after presentation, except that any bill amended and reenacted within 10 days preceding the expiration of the second legislative year shall become law only if the Governor signs it prior to noon of the seventh day following such expiration. No bill shall be returned by the Governor a second time. No bill need be read three times and no emergency resolution need be adopted for the reenactment of any bill at a special session of the Legislature.

This paragraph contains the very important gubernatorial check on the legislature, the veto power. The 1776 Constitution contained no gubernatorial veto, and the 1844 provision, Article V, section 7, provided a "weak" veto that could be overridden by only a majority of the legislature. The item veto for appropriation bills was added by amendment in 1875, but was separated into the next paragraph by the 1947 Constitution. Also, the 1947 Constitution strengthened the veto power by requiring a two-thirds vote in the legislature to override a veto, and by adding the "conditional veto," now reflected in paragraph 14(f). The conditional veto permits the governor to return a bill to the legislature, together with recommendations without actually vetoing it (In re Application of McGlynn). Thereafter, if the legislature agrees, only a majority vote is needed to repass the bill rather than the two-thirds vote to override a veto. This form of executive-legislative interaction seems to have been a very valuable addition to the veto power.[41]

Until 1981 the governor could exercise a form of "pocket veto" because as a matter of legislative practice, although not required by the constitution, the legislature would not "present" a bill to him until he requested it. When used at the end of the second year of a legislative session, a governor's mere delay in requesting a bill could defeat a bill that had passed both houses. After a 1981 decision of the New Jersey Supreme Court declining to interfere with this practice on the ground that it was a nonjusticiable political question (Gilbert v. Gladden), an amendment was adopted to restructure the provision to eliminate this form of pocket veto by requiring in paragraph 14(a) the speedy presentment to the governor.

The New Jersey Supreme Court has held that any attempt by the legislature, such as a "legislative veto" whereby the legislature purports to disapprove administrative rules by a resolution not "presented" to the governor, violates the requirement of paragraph 14(a) that laws be presented to the governor for his review (General Assembly v. Byrne).

> 15. If any bill presented to the Governor shall contain one or more items of appropriation of money, he may object in whole or in part to any such item or items while approving the other portions of the bill. In such case he shall append to the bill, at the time of signing it, a statement of each item or part thereof to which he objects, and each item or part so objected to shall not take effect. A copy of such statement shall be transmitted by him to the house in which the bill originated, and each item or part thereof objected to shall be separately reconsidered. If upon reconsideration, on or after the third day following said transmittal, one or more of such items or parts thereof be approved by two-thirds of all the members of each house, the same shall become a part of the law, notwithstanding the objections of the Governor. All the provisions of the preceding paragraph in relation to bills not approved by the Governor shall apply to cases in which he shall withhold his approval from any item or items or parts thereof contained in a bill appropriating money.

This "item veto" for appropriation bills was added by amendment in 1875 and was moved to this paragraph in 1947. Also, in 1947, the power to reduce items was included. Because the preexisting conventional veto was an "all-or-nothing" power, under which the governor must accept or reject entire legislative measures, this item veto power made an exception in the area of appropriation bills that permitted a more targeted, fine-tuned veto power to reduce or eliminate parts of appropriation bills. In other respects this item veto power is exercised in the same way and is subject to the same restrictions as set forth in paragraph 14.

In a major decision in 1984 (Karcher v. Kean), the New Jersey Supreme Court set forth a number of interpretations of this provision, including a definition of "appropriation":

An appropriation is an authorization, statutorily enacted by the Legislature, for the withdrawal of monies from the State treasury for governmental purposes. . . . There are, however, no specific constitutional standards or rules for determining the content or format of an appropriations act. Therefore, some inherent flexibility and discretion attend the fiscal-formulation process.

In Karcher the court upheld gubernatorial vetoes of conditions related to expenditure of funds and reductions in appropriated funds.

SECTION II

1. The Governor may grant pardons and reprieves in all cases other than impeachment and treason, and may suspend and remit fines and forfeitures. A commission or other body may be established by law to aid and advise the Governor in the exercise of executive clemency.

This provision has its origins in Article V, sections 9 and 10, of the Constitution of 1844. The last sentence was added in 1947, apparently to eliminate any separation of powers problems that might arise from statutes purporting to assist in this executive function.

The power to grant pardons and reprieves and to suspend and remit fines are exclusive executive powers, to be exercised after a defendant has been sentenced by the judiciary. Courts will not review the exercise or refusal to exercise executive clemency (State v. Mangino).

2. A system for the granting of parole shall be provided by law.

This paragraph, which had no counterpart in earlier constitutions, has been held not to create a constitutional right to parole (New Jersey State Parole Board v. Byrne). In the New Jersey State Parole Board decision, the New Jersey Supreme Court traced the history of parole in New Jersey and concluded that, as a matter of "fundamental fairness" but not as a matter of constitutional mandate, inmates were entitled to notice of the pendency of a parole hearing, any statements opposing parole, and an opportunity to respond in writing. Otherwise, although this paragraph requires the legislature to provide for a system of parole, the details of the system are a matter for legislative discretion (In re Parole Application of Trantino). Interestingly, this mandate to the legislature appears in the executive article of the constitution and separates the parole system, which is legislatively created and structured, from executive clemency.[42]

SECTION III

1. Provision for organizing, inducting, training, arming, disciplining and regulating a militia shall be made by law, which shall conform to applicable standards established for the armed forces of the United States.

This and the next paragraph concerning the militia have their origins in Articles VIII and X of the Constitution of 1776, together with Article VII of the 1844 Constitution, as amended in 1875. There is, of course, much less need for state constitutional treatment of the militia in modern times than in the past. This paragraph has not been the subject of significant judicial interpretation.

2. The Governor shall nominate and appoint all general and flag officers of the militia, with the advice and consent of the Senate. All other commissioned officers of the militia shall be appointed and commissioned by the Governor according to law.

See discussion under prior paragraph.

SECTION IV

1. All executive and administrative offices, departments, and instrumentalities of the State government, including the offices of Secretary of State and Attorney General, and their respective functions, powers and duties, shall be allocated by law among and within not more than twenty principal departments, in such manner as to group the same according to major purposes so far as practicable. Temporary commissions for special purposes may, however, be established by law and such commissions need not be allocated within a principal department.

This paragraph, new in 1947, when read together with the next paragraph making the principal departments of state government subject to gubernatorial supervision, forms the basis for a streamlined, modern, and accountable executive branch (Association of New Jersey State College Faculties, Inc. v. Board of Higher Education). The legislature still has the power to organize and allocate powers within the executive departments (Dalton v. Kean), but the legislature may delegate power to reorganize the executive departments to the governor (Brown v. Heymann). The final sentence permitting temporary commissions gives the legislature the flexibility to respond to specific problems without having to consider the permanent structure of the executive branch.

> 2. Each principal department shall be under the supervision of the Governor. The head of each principal department shall be a single executive unless otherwise provided by law. Such single executives shall be nominated and appointed by the Governor, with the advice and consent of the Senate, to serve at the pleasure of the Governor during his term of office and until the appointment and qualification of their successors, except as herein otherwise provided with respect to the Secretary of State and Attorney General.

This paragraph, also new in 1947, is aimed at pinpointing responsibility and control within the executive branch. Not only are department heads under the governor's supervision and serve at his pleasure after being appointed by him, but they are to be individuals rather than boards or commissions unless the legislature decides otherwise. This provision ended the proliferation of independent boards and agencies that had occurred prior to 1947 (Sprissler v. Pennsylvania-Reading Seashore Lines). In the Sprissler case, the New Jersey Supreme Court rejected an attack, based on this provision, on statutes that granted authority over railroads to two different departments.

> 3. The Secretary of State and the Attorney General shall be nominated and appointed by the Governor with the advice and consent of the Senate to serve during the term of office of the Governor.

This paragraph, based on Article XII of the 1776 Constitution and Article VII, section 2, paragraph 4, of the 1844 Constitution, as amended in 1875, establishes the secretary of state and attorney general as the only statewide constitutional executive officers other than the governor, but still makes them appointed by the governor with advice and consent of the senate. These two officers, however, do not serve at the pleasure of the governor, but rather have set terms of office that coincide with the governor. Although the attorney general is a constitutional officer, virtually all of his powers and duties as the chief legal officer of the state emanate from the common law and statutes (Van Riper v. Jenkins).

The New Jersey Constitution is unusual among state constitutions in that the governor is the only official elected on a statewide basis. This pinpoints responsibility for executive branch operations in the governor's office and also adds to his power. Provisions such as this one implement the powerful governor approach.

> 4. Whenever a board, commission or other body shall be the head of a principal department, the members thereof shall be nominated and appointed

by the Governor with the advice and consent of the Senate, and may be removed in the manner provided by law. Such a board, commission or other body may appoint a principal executive officer when authorized by law, but the appointment shall be subject to the approval of the Governor. Any principal executive officer so appointed shall be removable by the Governor, upon notice and an opportunity to be heard.

This paragraph governs situations where department heads are not single individuals, but rather are boards or commissions. The approach obviously gives the governor direct control over these types of departments, as well as those headed by an individual. This paragraph has not been the subject of judicial interpretation.

5. The Governor may cause an investigation to be made of the conduct in office of any officer or employee who receives his compensation from the State of New Jersey, except a member, officer or employee of the Legislature or an officer elected by the Senate and General Assembly in joint meeting, or a judicial officer. He may require such officers or employees to submit to him a written statement or statements, under oath, of such information as he may call for relating to the conduct of their respective offices or employments. After notice, the service of charges and an opportunity to be heard at public hearing the Governor may remove any such officer or employee for cause. Such officer or employee shall have the right of judicial review, on both the law and the facts, in such manner as shall be provided by law.

This paragraph, new in 1947, gives the governor the power to investigate the conduct of executive branch officials and to discipline them, while respecting, on separation of powers grounds, the legislative and judicial branches. Also, the provision requires cause for removal and specifies procedural protections such as notice, hearing, and judicial review (Russo v. Meyner). In Russo, the New Jersey Supreme Court held that the governor's power to remove state officers and employees carried with it, inherently, "the right to impose all lesser degrees of punishment." The Appellate Division has held that such lesser degrees of punishment, such as suspension, are not within the exclusive power of the governor, but may also be imposed by department heads (Grzankowski v. Heymann).

6. No rule or regulation made by any department, officer, agency or authority of this state, except such as relates to the organization or internal management of the State government or a part thereof, shall take effect until it is filed either with the Secretary of State or in such other manner as may be provided by law. The Legislature shall provide for the prompt publication of such rules and regulations.

This paragraph, new in 1947, is intended to provide at least minimal notice to the public of administrative rules and regulations. In 1953 the Appellate

Division held that this provision was prospective and applied only to administrative rules and regulations adopted after the effective date of the 1947 Constitution (Frigiola v. State Board of Education). The paragraph is now implemented by the legislature by the Administrative Procedure Act.[43]

Article VI

Judicial

SECTION I

1. The judicial power shall be vested in a Supreme Court, a Superior Court, and other courts of limited jurisdiction. The other courts and their jurisdiction may from time to time be established, altered or abolished by law.

In relatively simple terms, this provision assigns the "judicial power," as opposed to legislative and executive power, to the courts. The constitution sets up a unified court system—a judiciary under a single administrative head, with the same types of courts throughout the state. This paragraph is based on Article VI, section 1, of the 1844 Constitution. Prior to a 1978 amendment the paragraph required county courts and referred to "inferior" courts rather than the current language of "other" courts.

The New Jersey Supreme Court has held in State v. Abbati that:

The constitutional judicial power embraces ancillary inherent powers. The inherent powers of our courts are not defined by the judicial article, and any exhaustive definition of these powers is practically impossible. . . . The judicial article reposes in our courts the power to create, mold and apply remedies once jurisdiction is invoked.

In the Abbati decision the Court concluded that a trial court could dismiss an indictment after two mistrials based on deadlocked juries, even though not required to do so on double jeopardy grounds.

The New Jersey Supreme Court has noted that its judicial power does not extend to "political questions" that are "nonjusticiable" (Gilbert v. Gladden).

Even though the judicial article does not include the requirement of a "case or controversy," like Article III of the federal Constitution, the New Jersey courts still impose a requirement of standing (sufficient interest in the outcome of the litigation) before litigants may invoke the judicial power of the courts, but this requirement does not have to meet federal standards (Salorio v. Glaser). The courts will not "render advisory opinions or function in the abstract . . . nor will we entertain proceedings by plaintiffs who are 'mere intermeddlers' . . . or are merely interlopers or strangers to the dispute" (Crescent Park Tenants Association v. Realty Equities Corp.). In Crescent Park the Court stated, however, that "New Jersey cases have historically taken a much more liberal approach on the issue of standing than have the federal cases."

The New Jersey Supreme Court has even gone so far as to decide cases that are "moot," or in which there is no longer a live controversy, where "the public interest warrants a resolution of the cause" (John F. Kennedy Memorial Hospital v. Heston). Although standing of nonprofit associations to litigate questions in which their members have an interest has generally been upheld, the rights of such associations or their members must be affected before a court will adjudicate a controversy (In re Association of Trial Lawyers of America).

The Supreme Court has broad powers over the administration of the court system (In re Waiver of the Death Penalty).

SECTION II

1. The Supreme Court shall consist of a Chief Justice and six Associate Justices. Five members of the court shall constitute a quorum. When necessary, the Chief Justice shall assign the Judge or Judges of the Superior Court, senior in service, as provided by rules of the Supreme Court, to serve temporarily in the Supreme Court. In case the Chief Justice is absent or unable to serve, a presiding Justice designated in accordance with rules of the Supreme Court shall serve temporarily in his stead.

This paragraph replaced the earlier Court of Errors and Appeals and Supreme Court with a single Supreme Court of seven justices, five of whom shall constitute a quorum. It gives the chief justice the flexibility to utilize retired Superior Court judges to sit on the Supreme Court.

2. The Supreme Court shall exercise appellate jurisdiction in the last resort in all causes provided in this Constitution.

This paragraph, referring to the Supreme Court's appellate jurisdiction, must be read together with Article VI, Section V, paragraph 1, which delineates the Supreme Court's appellate jurisdiction.

> 3. The Supreme Court shall make rules governing the administration of all courts in the State and, subject to the law, the practice and procedure in all such courts. The Supreme Court shall have jurisdiction over the admission to the practice of law and the discipline of persons admitted.

This paragraph, new in 1947, assigns very important powers to the Supreme Court outside the context of adjudicating cases. The Court has rulemaking power over the areas of judicial administration and practice and procedure in the courts. Further, it has jurisdiction over the legal profession. These grants of power to the Supreme Court act as limits on legislative power in these areas.

Within two years of this provision taking effect, the question of the meaning of "subject to law" in relation to rules of practice and procedure arose. In Winberry v. Salisbury the New Jersey Supreme Court held that this phrase referred only to substantive law, and that in the area of practice and procedure the Court's rulemaking power was exclusive and the legislature therefore could not pass laws relating to practice and procedure. This decision drew nationwide attention.[44]

The Supreme Court has been very active in its use of the rulemaking power. For example, in 1973 it concluded that, with respect to the matter of the payment of interest on tort judgments that accrues before the judgment is entered, the Court could require the payment of such interest even if it were viewed as substantive law and not practice and procedure (Busik v. Levine). In Busik the Court noted that it sometimes deals with questions of practice and procedure in its decisions in adjudicated cases and later promulgates the same result in a court rule. The Court concluded:

The constitutional grant of rule-making power as to practice and procedure is simply a grant of power; it would be a mistake to find in that grant restrictions upon judicial techniques for the exercise of that power, and a still larger mistake to suppose that the grant of that power impliedly deprives the judiciary of flexibility in the area called "substantive" law.

The Court has read its power over practice and procedure broadly to include, for example, the creation by court rule of a pretrial intervention program (State v. Leondaris).

The Court's power to "make rules governing the administration of courts in the state" has also been read broadly to support judicial supervision of probation officers, which transcends statutes governing public employees (Passaic County Probation Officers' Association v. County of Passaic). It has further held that this power over judicial administration gives the Court the "power to compel the appropriation of funds and the employment of personnel necessary for the efficient administration of justice" (In re Court Budget and Court Personnel in Essex County; In re County of Hudson 1982 Judicial Budget Impasse). On the other hand, the Court has upheld conflict-of-interest legislation, as applied to judges, despite the argument that it conflicted with the Court's constitutional power over administration of the courts (Knight v. City of Margate). There, the Court emphasized the need for cooperation among the branches of government.

Finally, this paragraph grants the Supreme Court "jurisdiction over the admission to the practice of law and the discipline of persons admitted." This grant of power to the Court limits the legislature's authority with respect to lawyers and the practice of law. Therefore, the qualifications, ethics, and discipline of lawyers, and matters relating to unauthorized practice of law, are matters for court rules. The Supreme Court has held that its power in this area is exclusive (State v. Rush). It has also interpreted the power broadly to protect the public (In re Boyle) by, for example, adopting a rule limiting lawyers' contingent fees in personal injury cases (American Trial Lawyers Association v. New Jersey Supreme Court), providing confidentiality for those who file ethics complaints against lawyers (In re Hearing on Immunity for Ethics Complainants), and setting up committees to arbitrate fee disputes between lawyers and clients (In re LiVolsi). The Court has disciplined lawyers for public disrespect of the judicial system (In re Hinds) and has held that a judge formerly removed from the bench under Article VI, Section VI, paragraph 6 may also, in his capacity as a lawyer, be disciplined under this paragraph (Matter of Yaccarino [1989]).

The Supreme Court Rules, in which the Court has implemented these various rulemaking powers, are published and available.[45]

SECTION III

> 1. The Superior Court shall consist of such number of judges as may be authorized by law, each of whom shall exercise the powers of the court subject to rules of the Supreme Court. The Superior Court shall at all times consist of at least two judges who shall be assigned to sit in each of the counties of this State, and who are resident therein at the time of appointment and reappointment.

This paragraph implements an integral part of the 1947 Constitution's reform of the judiciary—a single, statewide court, created by the constitution, under the Supreme Court (O'Neill v. Vreeland). This reduces disputes over the jurisdiction of the courts, because this single Superior Court has statewide jurisdiction as specified in the next paragraph. The last sentence was added by amendment in 1978.

> 2. The Superior Court shall have original general jurisdiction throughout the State in all causes.

This paragraph, to be read with the preceding paragraph, assigns statewide jurisdiction to the Superior Court in "all causes," including criminal and civil cases. Thus, this is the constitutionally created court of general jurisdiction in New Jersey. This merged the former distinction between law and equity into a single court, avoiding multiple trials (Asbestos Fibres, Inc. v. Martin Laboratories, Inc.), while still preserving the dichotomy between jury questions (law) and judge questions (equity).

> 3. The Superior Court shall be divided into an Appellate Division, a Law Division and a Chancery Division, which shall include a family part. Each division shall have such other parts, consist of such number of judges, and hear such causes, as may be provided by rules of the Supreme Court. At least two judges of the Superior Court shall at all times be assigned to sit in each of the counties of the State, who at the time of their appointment and reappointment were residents of that county provided, however, that the number of judges required to reside in the county wherein they sit shall be at least equal in number to the number of judges of the county court sitting in each of the counties at the adoption of this amendment.

This paragraph divides the single, statewide Superior Court into the three main divisions, which perform appellate and trial functions. It was amended in 1983 to require the Chancery Division to include a family part. The second sentence was added in 1978. The personnel of each division and the types of cases they hear are determined by the Supreme Court in its rulemaking capacity.

> 4. Subject to rules of the Supreme Court, the Law Division and the Chancery Division shall each exercise the powers and functions of the other division when the ends of justice so require, and legal and equitable relief shall be granted in any cause so that all matters in controversy between the parties may be completely determined.

This paragraph furthers the aim of simplifying the judicial system by providing that, pursuant to Supreme Court rules, each division may exercise the powers of the other where necessary. This permits a single law suit to resolve all the issues between the parties, even if they are both legal and equitable (Rolleri v. Lordi).

Also, the New Jersey Supreme Court has interpreted this provision to "constitutionalize" the entire controversy doctrine (Cogdell v. Hospital Center at Orange). The entire controversy doctrine requires a party having claims against a number of other persons to join all such claims in one lawsuit, or waive the right to sue parties not joined in the first suit. In Cogdell, the Supreme Court stated that "The purposes of the doctrine include the needs of economy and the avoidance of waste, efficiency and the reduction of delay, fairness to parties, and the need for complete and final disposition through the avoidance of 'peacemeal decisions.' "

SECTION IV

Article VI, Section IV repealed effective December 7, 1978.

This section, formerly providing for county courts, was repealed by amendment in 1978.

SECTION V

1. Appeals may be taken to the Supreme Court:

(a) In causes determined by the Appellate Division of the Superior Court involving a question arising under the Constitution of the United States or this State;

(b) In causes where there is a dissent in the Appellate Division of the Superior Court;

(c) In capital causes;

(d) On certification by the Supreme Court to the Superior Court and, where provided by rules of the Supreme Court, to the inferior courts; and

(e) In such causes as may provided by law.

This paragraph, to be read together with Article VI, Section II, paragraph 2, sets out the constitutionally mandated appellate jurisdiction of the Supreme Court, concluding with the authorization to the legislature to provide by law for additional appellate jurisdiction. Subparagraphs (a), (b), and (c) delineate categories of cases where a party may appeal as a matter of right—the Supreme Court's jurisdiction is not a matter for its own discretion. Subparagraph (a) gives jurisdiction over constitutional questions, but this has been read by the Supreme Court to require a *substantial* constitutional question, which normally should have been raised first in the lower courts (Deerfield Estates, Inc. v. Township of East Brunswick; Meeker v. Meeker). In the Deerfield case, however, the Supreme Court noted that, when in doubt, one who seeks to appeal as a matter of right should also petition for certification under subparagraph (d), addressed to the Court's discretionary appellate jurisdiction. The Court may treat cases that are appealed as though a petition for certification has been filed (Piscataway Associates, Inc. v. Township of Piscataway).

The Supreme Court has held that an appeal as a matter of right, under subparagraph (b) where there is a dissent in the Appellate Division, "is limited to those issues encompassed by the dissent," and other issues must be raised by way of petition for certification (Gilborges v. Wallace).

Subparagraph (c) provides a right to appeal in capital, or death penalty cases, and basically works to involve the Supreme Court in every death penalty case.

The Court will hear these appeals even where the defendant does not want to appeal (State v. Koedatich).

Subparagraph (d) sets forth the Supreme Court's discretionary certification procedure, which is governed by the Court's rules. A denial of certification by the Court is not considered as any type of ruling with respect to the decision of the lower court (West Point Island Civic Association v. Township Committee of Dover Township).

> 2. Appeals may be taken to the Appellate Division of the Superior Court from the law and chancery divisions of the Superior Court and in such other causes as may be provided by law.

This paragraph provides an appeal as a matter of right from the Law and Chancery divisions to the Appellate Division, and permits the legislature to provide other types of cases that may be appealed to the Appellate Division. In 1952 the Supreme Court noted in Midler v. Heinowitz:

> Our new judicial structure is modeled after the federal court system. Our system, too, contemplates one appeal as of right to a court of general appellate jurisdiction. This is afforded usually in the Appellate Division of the Superior Court. A further appeal to this court is allowed only in the exercise of our discretional power of certification unless the case comes within one of the limited number of situations for which an appeal to this court as of right is expressly allowed.

> 3. The Supreme Court and the Appellate Division of the Superior Court may exercise such original jurisdiction as may be necessary to the complete determination of any cause on review.

This paragraph concerns the original, as opposed to appellate, jurisdiction of the Supreme Court and the Appellate Division. Original jurisdiction refers to cases that may be filed in these courts in the first instance, rather than being brought as appeals from decisions already rendered by lower courts. The Supreme Court has held that this grant of original jurisdiction applies only to "matters related to causes already before us" (In re LiVolsi) and has resorted to this power to hear matters that have not been raised properly under its appellate jurisdiction (Kelly v. Curtiss).

> 4. Prerogative writs are superseded and, in lieu thereof, review, hearing and relief shall be afforded in the Superior Court, on terms and in the manner provided by rules of the Supreme Court, as of right, except in criminal causes where such review shall be discretionary.

This paragraph abolishes the prerogative writs (*prohibition, mandamus, quo warranto*) that were in use prior to the 1947 Constitution. Such writs, which were discretionary, were used by the courts to accomplish specific ends such as determining a person's right to hold public office (*quo warranto*), requiring an official to perform a nondiscretionary act (*mandamus*), or forbidding a lower court or agency from hearing a matter over which it did not have jurisdiction (*prohibition*).

Under this paragraph, relief may now be sought as a matter of right, in a single type of proceeding, without all the technical details of each of the prerogative writs. These actions are now known as actions "in lieu of prerogative writs." The main function of these proceedings is to guarantee the right to appeal from decisions of legislatively created administrative agencies (In re LiVolsi).

SECTION VI

1. The Governor shall nominate and appoint, with the advice and consent of the Senate, the Chief Justice and associate justices of the Supreme Court, the Judges of the Superior Court, and the judges of the inferior courts with jurisdiction extending to more than one municipality; except that upon the abolition of the juvenile and domestic relations courts or family court and county district courts as provided by law, the judges of those former courts shall become the Judges of the Superior Court without nomination by the Governor or confirmation by the Senate. No nomination to such an office shall be sent to the Senate for confirmation until after 7 days' public notice by the Governor.

This paragraph places the authority for appointment of judges with the governor. New Jersey has never had an elected judiciary. The last sentence guarantees at least seven days notice before judicial nominations are sent to the senate for confirmation. The practice of "senatorial courtesy," whereby the governor will not nominate a judge unless approved by the senator from the candidate's district, has played an important role in the "advice and consent" function of the senate on judicial nominations.[46] A recent suit to stop the system by which the governor solicits information on potential judicial nominees from the State Bar Association was dismissed as a nonjusticiable political question (Loigman v. Trombadore).

2. The justices of the Supreme Court and the judges of the Superior Court shall each prior to his appointment have been admitted to the practice of law in this State for at least 10 years.

This paragraph sets forth the requirement that Supreme Court justices and Superior Court judges be lawyers, who have been admitted to practice in New Jersey for at least ten years.

3. The Justices of the Supreme Court and the Judges of the Superior Court shall hold their offices for initial terms of 7 years and upon reappointment shall hold their offices during good behavior; provided however, that, upon the abolition of the juvenile and domestic relations courts or family court

and county district courts as provided by law, the judges in office in those former courts who have acquired tenure and the Judges of the Superior Court who have acquired tenure as a judge in those former courts prior to appointment to the Superior Court, shall have tenure as Judges of the Superior Court. Judges of the juvenile and domestic relations courts or family court and county district courts who have not acquired tenure as a judge of those former courts shall hold their offices for the period of their respective terms which remain unexpired and shall acquire tenure upon reappointment to the Superior Court. Such justices and judges shall be retired upon attaining the age of 70 years. Provisions for the pensioning of the Justices of the Supreme Court and the Judges of the Superior Court shall be made by law.

This paragraph sets up a basic seven-year term for Supreme Court justices and Superior Court judges. This may be followed by a possible reappointment by the governor, and after advice and consent by the senate, the judge would acquire "tenure" and stay in office "during good behavior" or until the mandatory retirement age of seventy. Thus, New Jersey, although providing for an appointed judiciary, does not follow the federal model of a single, lifetime appointment (Lloyd v. Vermeulen). The legislature is required to provide for judicial pensions.

4. The Justices of the Supreme Court and the Judges of the Superior Court shall be subject to impeachment, and any judicial officer impeached shall not exercise his office until acquitted. The Judges of the Superior Court shall also not be subject to removal from office by the Supreme Court for such causes and in such manner as shall be provided by law.

This paragraph sets up two mechanisms for removal of Supreme Court justices and Superior Court judges: 1) impeachment by the legislature (including the requirement that once a judicial officer is impeached by the house he may not exercise the duties of his office until he is acquitted in a senate trial), or 2) removal of Superior Court judges by the Supreme Court pursuant to guidelines laid down by the legislature. Article VI, section 3, paragraph 2, of the 1844 Constitution provided for impeachment of judges. The second basis for removal was added in 1947.

The impeachment procedure is governed by Article VII, Section III. The process of Supreme Court removal pursuant to legislative guidelines is much broader than impeachment (Matter of Hardt), and the Court could probably, pursuant to its powers over judicial administration and attorney discipline, exceed legislative requirements (In re Mattera; Matter of Coruzzi).

5. Whenever the Supreme Court shall certify to the Governor that it appears that any Justice of the Supreme Court or Judge of the Superior Court is so incapacitated as substantially to prevent him from performing his judicial duties, the Governor shall appoint a commission of three persons to inquire

into the circumstances; and, on their recommendation, the Governor may retire the justice or judge from office, on pension as may be provided by law.

This paragraph sets forth an alternative to the removal provisions of the preceding paragraph, for use when a judge has become incapacitated in office. Interestingly, it involves the governor in the process, and the final decision, if so recommended by a three-person gubernatorial committee, resides with the governor. This technique of removal results in a retirement with a pension. It has not been subject to judicial interpretation.

6. The Justices of the Supreme Court and the Judges of the Superior Court shall receive for their services such salaries as may be provided by law, which shall not be diminished during the term of their appointment. They shall not, while in office, engage in the practice of law or other gainful pursuit.

This paragraph sets forth the requirement that judicial salaries shall be set by law, but may not be diminished during a judge's term of office. The provision is based on Article VII, section 2, paragraph 1, of the 1844 Constitution.

The paragraph also contains a prohibition on judges practicing law or engaging in "other gainful pursuit." The Supreme Court has strictly enforced this restriction on other gainful pursuit (Matter of Yaccarino [1985]). In addition, the court has gone to great lengths to keep even the appearance of politics out of the judiciary, even for judicial employees other than judges (Matter of Randolph) and judicial spouses (In re Application of Gaulkin). In Randolph, the Court stated "One of the great reforms of the judicial article of the 1947 New Jersey Constitution was the complete separation of politics from the judiciary."

7. The Justices of the Supreme Court and the Judges of the Superior Court shall hold no other office or position, of profit, under this State or the United States. Any such justice or judge who shall become a candidate for an elective public office shall thereby forfeit his judicial office.

This paragraph is based on Article VII, section 2, paragraph 1, of the 1844 Constitution. It implements the separation of powers doctrine. The second sentence was added in 1947 to provide for the sanction of automatic forfeiture of judicial office. This prohibition, however, does not apply to surrogates, although they are judicial officers (Clark v. DeFino). The outcome of the DeFino case was subsequently changed when the Supreme Court changed its rules to prohibit surrogates from holding other political office (Pickett v. Harris).

SECTION VII

> 1. The Chief Justice of the Supreme Court shall be the administrative head of all the courts in the State. He shall appoint an Administrative Director to serve at his pleasure.

This paragraph establishes the chief justice as the administrative head of the unified court system. The 1947 Constitution's creation of a modern, streamlined, unified court system is further implemented by the authorization to the chief justice to appoint an administrative director to serve at his pleasure.[47] This provision created the first administrative office of the courts in any state.

> 2. The Chief Justice of the Supreme Court shall assign Judges of the Superior Court to the Divisions and Parts of the Superior Court, and may from time to time transfer Judges from one assignment to another, as need appears. Assignments to the Appellate Division shall be for terms fixed by rules of the Supreme Court.

This paragraph permits the chief justice to assign and transfer judges within the Superior Court, a power that further facilitates his authority over administration of the courts.

> 3. The Clerk of the Supreme Court and the Clerk of the Superior Court shall be appointed by the Supreme Court for such terms and at such compensation as shall be provided by law.

This paragraph revises Article VII, section 2, paragraph 4, of the 1844 Constitution, as renumbered paragraph 3 in 1875, which provided that Court clerks were appointed by the governor. Under the current provision the Supreme Court appoints the clerks, and their terms and compensation are set by the legislature.

Article VII

Public Officers and Employees

SECTION I

> 1. Every State officer, before entering upon the duties of his office, shall take and subscribe an oath or affirmation to support the Constitution of this State and of the United States and to perform the duties of his office faithfully, impartially and justly to the best of his ability.

This paragraph sets forth the required oath of office for state officers. In 1950 the New Jersey Supreme Court held that this constitutionally prescribed oath precluded the legislature from requiring an additional oath not to believe in the use of force or violence to overthrow the constitution nor to belong to organizations believing in such overthrow (Imbrie v. Marsh).

> 2. Appointments and promotions in the civil service of the State, and of such political subdivisions as may be provided by law, shall be made according to merit and fitness to be ascertained, as far as practicable, by examination, which, as far as practicable, shall be competitive; except that preference in appointments by reason of active service in any branch of the military or naval forces of the United States in time of war may be provided by law.

This paragraph requires, as a matter of constitutional mandate, a state civil service system, including political subdivisions to the extent required by the legislature. The provision "merely wrote into the state charter what had for years been the keystone of New Jersey's personnel system" (Bayonne v. Dougherty). The courts have recognized a number of exceptions to the requirements of this provision, such as authorizations to mayors to appoint police chiefs, based on its qualifier, "as far as practicable" (Newark Superior Officers Association v. City of Newark). Finally, the Supreme Court has noted that the purpose behind the merit and fitness requirement is to achieve efficient public service without political control and favoritism (O'Malley v. Department of Energy).

The provision includes an exception for veterans' preference. In Ballou v. State Department of Civil Service, the New Jersey Supreme Court noted: "A balance, not necessarily an equipoise, was struck in our Constitution between the competing values of a merit system and a veterans' preference system."

> 3. Any compensation for services or any fees received by any person by virtue of an appointive State office or position, in addition to the annual salary provided for the office or position, shall immediately upon receipt be paid into the treasury of the State, unless the compensation or fees shall be allowed or appropriated to him by law.

This paragraph provides that the annual salary for services in an appointive state position is the exclusive compensation, and any other fees or compensation shall be paid to the state treasury unless otherwise provided by the legislature.

> 4. Any person before or after entering upon the duties of any public office, position or employment in this State may be required to give bond as may be provided by law.

This paragraph authorizes the legislature to require various public officers or employees to be bonded or insured against their wrongful actions in office.

> 5. The term of office of all officers elected or appointed pursuant to the provisions of this Constitution, except as herein otherwise provided, shall commence on the day of the date of their respective commissions; but no commission for any office shall bear date prior to the expiration of the term of the incumbent of said office.

This paragraph is based on Article VII, section 2, paragraph 11, of the 1844 Constitution, as renumbered paragraph 10 in 1875. It sets forth a rule to determine the running of terms of office, which is from the date the governor grants the commission pursuant to his power under Article V, Section I, paragraph 12.

> 6. The State Auditor shall be appointed by the Senate and General Assembly in joint meeting for a term of five years and until his successor shall be appointed and qualified. It shall be his duty to conduct post-audits of all transactions and accounts kept by or for all departments, offices and agencies of the State government, to report to the Legislature or to any committee thereof as shall be required by law, and to perform such other similar or related duties as shall, from time to time, be required of him by law.

This paragraph provides for the only state official to be appointed by the legislature, the state auditor. This appointment is an express exception in Article IV, Section V, paragraph 5. The state auditor, answerable to the legislature, performs the auditing functions for the expenditure of state funds pursuant to legislative appropriations. Under Article VIII, section 1, of the 1844 Constitution, these functions were performed by the secretary of state, who was appointed by the legislature pursuant to Article VII, section 2, paragraph 3.

SECTION II

1. County prosecutors shall be nominated and appointed by the Governor with the advice and consent of the Senate. Their term of office shall be five years, and they shall serve until the appointment and qualification of their respective successors.

This paragraph is based on Article VII, section 2, paragraph 3, of the 1844 Constitution, which provided that ''prosecutors of pleas'' were appointed by the governor, with advice and consent of the senate. This current provision establishes the county prosecutors as constitutional officers with set terms of office. They operate with relative autonomy, even with respect to the attorney general (Morss v. Forbes). In Morss, the Supreme Court noted that ''it is evident that the jurisdiction of the county prosecutor has been carved out of the original powers of the attorney-general.'' Furthermore, county prosecutors are treated in this article on ''Public Officers and Employees'' rather than in the executive article, as is the attorney general.

2. County clerks, surrogates and sheriffs shall be elected by the people of their respective counties at general elections. The term of office of county clerks and surrogates shall be five years, and of sheriffs three years. Whenever a vacancy shall occur in any such office it shall be filled in the manner to be provided by law.

This paragraph is based on Article V, paragraph 12, and Article VII, section 2, paragraphs 6 and 7, of the 1844 Constitution. The provision establishes the offices of county clerk, surrogate, and sheriff as elected, constitutional officers for set terms of office.

Surrogates, who have jurisdiction over probating of wills and related matters, are judicial officers subject to the Code of Judicial Conduct (Pickett v. Harris). Although sheriffs are constitutional officers, the office of sheriff is a part of county government and subject to statutory regulation (Application of Burlington County Board of Chosen Freeholders).

SECTION III

> 1. The Governor and all other State officers, while in office and for two
> years thereafter, shall be liable to impeachment for misdemeanor committed
> during their respective continuance in office.

This paragraph specifies the officials, in addition to the judges covered under
Article VI, Section VI, paragraph 5, who will be subject to the legislature's
impeachment power under the next paragraph. It is based on basically the same
provisions in Article V, paragraph 11, of the 1844 Constitution. The provision
is fairly narrowly written to permit impeachment only for commission of "misdemeanor," but extends the officer's liability to impeachment to include the two
years after leaving office. Thus, a state officer may be impeached after leaving
office. There is virtually no judicial definition of "misdemeanor" except an
Appellate Division statement that practicing law while sitting as a judge of
compensation is not a misdemeanor (Bonafield v. Cahill).
A trial court has expressed the opinion that legislators are "State officers"
under this provision, and therefore may be liable to impeachment in addition to
the method of removal specified in Article IV, Section IV, paragraph 3 (State
v. Musto).

> 2. The General Assembly shall have the sole power of impeachment by
> vote of a majority of all the members. All impeachments shall be tried by
> the Senate, and members, when sitting for that purpose, shall be on oath or
> affirmation "truly and impartially to try and determine the charge in question
> according to the evidence." No person shall be convicted without the con-
> currence of two-thirds of all the members of the Senate. When the Governor
> is tried, the Chief Justice of the Supreme Court shall preside and the President
> of the Senate shall not participate in the trial.

This paragraph sets forth the basic, American model of the impeachment
process, with impeachment by the house, and trial in the senate with an extraordinary majority required for conviction. The provision has its origins in Article
XII of the 1776 Constitution, and Article VI, section 3, paragraph 1, of the 1844
Constitution. The last sentence was added in 1947.

> 3. Judgment in cases of impeachment shall not extend further than to
> removal from office, and to disqualification to hold and enjoy any public
> office of honor, profit or trust in this State; but the person convicted shall
> nevertheless be liable to indictment, trial and punishment according to law.

This paragraph, based on Article VI, section 3, paragraph 3, of the 1844
Constitution, presents the clear distinction between the remedy for impeachment
(removal and disqualification from office) and a criminal prosecution for crimes
committed in office. The former does not preclude the latter (In re Mattera).

Article VIII

Taxation and Finance

SECTION I

1. (a) Property shall be assessed for taxation under general laws and by uniform rules. All real property assessed and taxed locally or by the State for allotment and payment to taxing districts shall be assessed according to the same standard of value, except as otherwise permitted herein, and such real property shall be taxed at the general tax rate of the taxing district in which the property is situated, for the use of such taxing district.

(b) The Legislature shall enact laws to provide that the value of land, not less than 5 acres in area, which is determined by the assessing officer of the taxing jurisdiction to be actively devoted to agricultural or horticultural use and to have been so devoted for at least the 2 successive years immediately preceding the tax year in issue, shall, for local tax purposes, on application of the owner, be that value which such land has for agricultural or horticultural use.

Any such laws shall provide that when land which has been valued in this manner for local tax purposes is applied to a use other than for agriculture or horticulture it shall be subject to additional taxes in an amount equal to the difference, if any, between the taxes paid or payable on the basis of the valuation and the assessment authorized hereunder and the taxes that would have been paid or payable had the land been valued and assessed as otherwise provided in this Constitution, in the current year and in such of the tax years immediately preceding, not in excess of 2 such years in which the land was valued as herein authorized.

Such laws shall also provide for the equalization of assessments of land valued in accordance with the provisions hereof and for the assessment and collection of any additional taxes levied thereupon and shall include such other provisions as shall be necessary to carry out the provisions of this amendment.

Prior to 1875 the constitution did not contain limitations on the taxing power. In that year Article IV, section 7, paragraph 12, was added, which read simply: "Property shall be assessed for taxes under general laws, and by uniform rules, according to its true value." The provision was aimed at establishing a uniform system of property taxation, where property would be assessed equally in taxing districts because of the "true value" requirement, and as avoiding preferential taxation, particularly for railroads (New Jersey State League of Municipalities v. Kimmelman).

In the 1947 Constitution, matters of taxation and finance were brought together in a single article of the constitution, Article VIII. This paragraph replaced the "true value" requirement with "the same standard of value," a measure likewise aimed at equal assessments resulting in similar properties bearing a similar share of the tax burden (Robinson v. Cahill). Also, the 1947 version of this paragraph required real property to be taxed at "the general rate of the taxing district . . . for the use of such taxing district." These matters were among the most controversial of the constitutional debates of the 1940s.[48]

In 1962 the New Jersey Supreme Court ruled that a statute providing for the assessment of agricultural property at its value only for that use violated this paragraph's mandate that property be assessed according to the *same* standard of value (Switz v. Kingsley). As a result, an amendment was adopted in 1963, which inserted the exceptions for agricultural and horticultural property now reflected in subparagraph (b).[49]

The New Jersey Supreme Court has held that the basic uniformity requirement of this paragraph applies only to property taxes and not to excise taxes (Foosaner v. Director, Division of Taxation).

The New Jersey Supreme Court noted in Switz v. Township of Middletown concerning the uniformity provisions of this paragraph: "The dominant principle of the new constitutional mandate is equality of treatment and burden; and this was the genius and spirit of the old provision as well." The Court has enforced the uniformity principle strictly, providing effective remedies for taxpayers who demonstrate their property is not being taxed uniformly (Switz v. Township of Middletown; In re Appeals of Kents). The Court has also struck down statutes providing that unoccupied, residential housing shall not be taxed (New Jersey State League of Municipalities v. Kimmelman) and refused to permit reductions in assessed value of property attributable to the costs of cleaning up environmental damage (Inmar Associates, Inc. v. Borough of Carlstalt).

2. Exemption from taxation may be granted only by general laws. Until otherwise provided by law all exemptions from taxation validly granted and now in existence shall be continued. Exemptions from taxation may be altered or repealed, except those exempting real and personal property used

exclusively for religious, educational, charitable or cemetery purposes, as defined by law, and owned by any corporation or association organized and conducted exclusively for one or more of such purposes and not operating for profit.

This paragraph, new in 1947, governs tax exemptions by limiting the legislative grant of tax exemptions to general laws. (See also Article IV, Section VII, paragraph 9(6), prohibiting special laws relating to "taxation or exemption therefrom"). It further constitutionalized the tax exemptions in existence in 1947 (New Jersey League of Municipalities v. Kimmelman), as well as protected the exemption of property used exclusively for religious, educational, charitable, and cemetery purposes from legislative repeal. Even before this paragraph was adopted, the New Jersey courts recognized the legislature's power to grant tax exemptions, despite the 1875 uniformity provision (General Electric Co. v. City of Passaic).

The key focus in evaluating tax exemptions is on the use to which the property is put, rather than on the status of the owner (New Jersey Turnpike Authority v. Washington Township). In Washington Township Chief Justice Vanderbilt stated:

The taxing power lies at the heart of government. Without taxes the government could not function. Any impairment of the taxing power affects the lifeblood of government. Accordingly claims for tax exemption have to stand scrutiny to show that they serve a public purpose.

The courts have upheld a statutory date of October 1 for determining the exempt status of property and have thus denied exemption to property transferred to exempt use after that date (Bethany Baptist Church v. Deptford Township). The constitutional requirement that tax exemptions be granted only by general laws means that "a tax exemption statute must draw classifications which rest upon 'substantial distinctions' that have a 'logical and reasonable basis,' and include all property falling within the named classification" (General Electric Co. v. City of Passaic).

This paragraph permits tax exemptions to be granted by the legislature. Therefore, many New Jersey tax exemption cases focus on statutory interpretation. The statutes are construed strictly, to avoid undermining the state's taxing power, and the burden of proof rests on those claiming a tax exemption (Presbyterian Homes v. Division of Tax Appeals).

3. Any citizen and resident of this state now or hereafter honorably discharged or released under honorable circumstances from active service, in time of war or other emergency as, from time to time, defined by the Legislature, in any branch of the Armed Forces of the United States shall be entitled, annually to a deduction from the amount of any tax bill for taxes on real and personal property, or both, including taxes attributable to a

residential unit held by a stockholder in a cooperative or mutual housing corporation, in the sum of $50.00 or if the amount of any such tax bill shall be less than $50.00, to a cancellation thereof, which deduction or cancellation shall not be altered or repealed. Any person hereinabove described who has been or shall be declared by the United States Veterans Administration, or its successor, to have a service-connected disability, shall be entitled to such further deduction from taxation as from time to time may be provided by law. The surviving spouse of any citizen and resident of this State who has met or shall meet his or her death on active duty in time of war or of other emergency as so defined in any such service shall be entitled, during her widowhood or his widowerhood, as the case may be, and while a resident of this State, to the deduction or cancellation in this paragraph provided for honorably discharged veterans and to such further deduction as from time to time may be provided by law. The surviving spouse of any citizen and resident of this State who has had or shall hereafter have active service in time of war or of other emergency as so defined in any branch of the Armed Forces of the United States and who died or shall die while on active duty in any branch of the Armed Forces of the United States, or who has been or may hereafter be honorably discharged or released under honorable circumstances from active service in time of war or of other emergency as so defined in any branch of the Armed Forces of the United States shall be entitled, during her widowhood or his widowerhood, as the case may be, and while a resident of this State, to the deduction or cancellation in this paragraph provided for honorably discharged veterans and to such further deductions as from time to time may be provided by law.

This paragraph, also new in 1947, was intended to provide a constitutionally mandated tax deduction or exemption for veterans. It was amended in 1953, 1963, 1983, and 1988, each time to expand its coverage. The paragraph's limitation to widows prior to the 1983 amendment was held to discriminate against widowers, in violation of the federal Constitution (Borough of Wrightstown v. Medved). The intent of the veteran's tax deduction was "to compensate veterans for the experiences of war and to encourage veterans to purchase property in this State," and therefore was properly denied to a conscientious objector (Darnell v. Township of Moorestown).

4. The Legislature may, from time to time, enact laws granting an annual deduction, from the amount of any tax bill for taxes on the real property, and from taxes attributable to a residential unit in a cooperative or mutual housing corporation, of any citizen and resident of this State of the age of 65 or more years, or any citizen and resident of this State less than 65 years of age who is permanently and totally disabled according to the provisions of the Federal Social Security Act, residing in a dwelling house owned by him which is a constituent part of such real property, or residing in a dwelling house owned by him which is assessed as a real property but which is situated on land owned by another or others, or residing as tenant—shareholder in a cooperative or mutual housing corporation, but no such deduction shall be in excess of $160.00 with respect to any year prior to 1981, $200.00

per year in 1981, $225.00 per year in 1982, and $250.00 per year in 1983 and any year thereafter and such deduction shall be restricted to owners having an income not in excess of $5,000.00 per year with respect to any year prior to 1981, $8,000.00 per year in 1981, $9,000.00 per year in 1982, and $10,000.00 per year in 1983 and any year thereafter, exclusive of benefits under any one of the following:

a. The Federal Social Security Act and all amendments and supplements thereto;

b. Any other program of the federal government or pursuant to any other federal law which provides benefits in whole or in part in lieu of benefits referred to in, or for persons excluded from coverage under, a. hereof including but not limited to the Federal Railroad Retirement Act and federal pension, disability and retirement programs; or

c. Pension, disability or retirement programs of any state or its political subdivisions, or agencies thereof, for persons not covered under a. hereof; provided, however, that the total amount of benefits to be allowed exclusion by any owner under b. or c. hereof shall not be in excess of the maximum amount of benefits payable to, and allowable for exclusion by, an owner in similar circumstances under a. hereof.

The surviving spouse of a deceased citizen and resident of this State who during his or her life received a deduction pursuant to this paragraph shall be entitled, so long as he or she shall remain unmarried and a resident of the same dwelling house situated on the same land with respect to which said deduction was granted, to the same deduction, upon the same conditions, with respect to the same real property or with respect to the same dwelling house which is situated on land owned by another or others, or with respect to the same cooperative or mutual housing corporation, notwithstanding that said surviving spouse is under the age of 65 and is not permanently and totally disabled, provided that said surviving spouse is 55 years of age or older.

Any such deduction when so granted by law shall be granted so that it will not be in addition to any other deduction or exemption, except a deduction granted under authority of paragraph 3 of this section, to which the said citizen and resident may be entitled, but said citizen and resident may receive in addition any homestead rebate or credit provided by law. The State shall annually reimburse each taxing district in an amount equal to one-half of the tax loss to the district resulting from the allowance of deductions pursuant to this paragraph.

This paragraph was added to the constitution by amendment in 1960, and, because of its detail, has had to be amended a number of times over the years. Amendments in 1963, 1970, 1971, 1975, 1980, 1984, and 1988 were aimed at increasing the dollar amounts of the deductions, expanding the types of property to which the tax deduction applies, excluding certain benefits from income eligibility levels, and indicating that both the veteran's deduction under paragraph 3 and this senior citizen's deduction may be claimed by an individual. The paragraph has not been subject to significant judicial interpretation.

> 5. The Legislature may adopt a homestead statute which entitles home-owners, residential tenants and net lease residential tenants to a rebate or a credit of a sum of money related to property taxes paid by or allocable to them at such rates and subject to such limits as may be provided by law. Such rebates or credits may include a differential rebate or credit to citizens and residents who are of the age of 65 or more years, or less than 65 years of age who are permanently and totally disabled according to the provisions of the Federal Social Security Act, or are 55 years of age or more and the surviving spouse of a deceased citizen or resident of this State who during his lifetime received, or who, upon the adoption of this amendment and the enactment of implementing legislation, would have been entitled to receive a rebate or credit related to property taxes.

This paragraph was added to the constitution by amendment in 1975 and then was amended in 1976 to permit higher rebates to senior citizens and persons with total and permanent disabilities. The New Jersey Supreme Court has upheld the statute implementing this paragraph, which limits eligibility for rebates to taxpayers' principal residences, thereby excluding summer homes. The Court concluded that this limitation was permitted by the word "homestead" in the constitutional provision (Rubin v. Glaser).

> 6. The Legislature may enact general laws under which municipalities may adopt ordinances granting exemptions or abatements from taxation on buildings and structures in areas declared in need of rehabilitation in accordance with statutory criteria, within such municipalities and to the land comprising the premises upon which such buildings or structures are erected and which is necessary for the fair enjoyment thereof. Such exemptions shall be for limited periods of time as specified by law, but not in excess of 5 years.

This paragraph, like paragraph 5, was added to the constitution by amendment in 1975. It permits the legislature to delegate to municipalities the power to grant up to five-year tax exemptions and abatements for buildings in areas in need of rehabilitation. It has not been subject to judicial interpretation.

> 7. No tax shall be levied on personal incomes of individuals, estates and trusts of this State unless the entire net receipts therefrom shall be received into the treasury, placed in a perpetual fund and be annually appropriated, pursuant to formulas established from time to time by the Legislature, to the several counties, municipalities and school districts of this State exclusively for the purpose of reducing or offsetting property taxes. In no event,

however, shall a tax so levied on personal incomes be levied on payments received under the federal Social Security Act, the federal Railroad Retirement Act, or any federal law which substantially reenacts the provisions of either of those laws.

This paragraph was added to the constitution by amendment in 1976. The prohibition on taxing the benefits listed in the last sentence was added by amendment in 1984. The basic thrust of the 1976 provision was to require that any personal income tax statute earmark revenues for offsetting or reduction of local property taxes, such as school taxes. This was part of the response to the crisis in education funding brought about by the ongoing Robinson v. Cahill litigation. See discussion under Article VIII, Section IV, paragraph 1. This paragraph has not been subject to judicial interpretation.

SECTION II

1. The credit of the State shall not be directly or indirectly loaned in any case.

This paragraph was carried over verbatim from Article IV, section 6, paragraph 3, of the 1844 Constitution. The provision was aimed at limiting the state from embarking on joint ventures with, or subsidizing projects of, private individuals or corporations.[50] This paragraph should be read together with Article VIII, Section III, paragraphs 2 and 3, which were designed to place similar limitations on local governments.

The New Jersey Supreme Court noted the purpose of these provisions in Roe v. Kervick:

During the nineteenth century states and their political subdivisions frequently undertook to encourage the development of railroads by furnishing financial aid. Such assistance was in the form of direct loans or gifts of public money or property, or by bond issues, or subscription to stock of the companies. Many abuses followed in the wake of such practices to the serious detriment of the taxpayer.

The strictures of *Article* VIII . . . were simply the retreat to a fundamental doctrine of government, *i.e.*, that public money should be raised and used only for public purposes.

The Court in Kervick went on to articulate the "public purpose" doctrine as permitting involvement in projects which benefit "the community as a whole." Further, the doctrine "must expand when necessary to encompass changing public needs in a modern dynamic society." The Court then approved state and local loans for Area Redevelopment Assistance projects.

Applying these views the Court has upheld a variety of public purpose projects despite the apparent rigid ban in this paragraph (Bulman v. McCrane).

2. No money shall be drawn from the State treasury but for appropriations made by law. All moneys for the support of the State government and for all other State purposes as far as can be ascertained or reasonably foreseen, shall be provided for in one general appropriation law covering one and the same fiscal year; except that when a change in the fiscal year is made, necessary provision may be made to effect the transition. No general appropriation law or other law appropriating money for any State purpose shall be enacted if the appropriation contained therein, together with all prior appropriations made for the same fiscal period, shall exceed the total amount of revenue on hand and anticipated which will be available to meet such appropriations during such fiscal period, as certified by the Governor.

This paragraph has its origins in Article IV, section 6, paragraph 2, of the 1844 Constitution, which contained the first sentence of the current provision. The rest of the provision was added by the 1947 Constitution.

The first sentence recognizes that the power to appropriate money is a legislative power (Karcher v. Kean). The 1947 additions establish the important policy requirements of a single, annual appropriation bill and a balanced budget (City of Camden v. Byrne).

3. The Legislature shall not, in any manner, create in any fiscal year a debt or debts, liability or liabilities of the State, which together with any previous debts or liabilities shall exceed at any time one per centum of the total amount appropriated by the general appropriation law for that fiscal year, unless the same shall be authorized by a law for some single object or work distinctly specified therein. Regardless of any limitation relating to taxation in this Constitution, such law shall provide the ways and means, exclusive of loans, to pay the interest of such debt or liability as it falls due, and also to pay and discharge the principal thereof within thirty-five years from the time it is contracted; and the law shall not be repealed until such debt or liability and the interest thereon are fully paid and discharged.

Except as hereinafter provided, no such law shall take effect until it shall have been submitted to the people at a general election and approved by a majority of the legally qualified voters of the State voting thereon. No voter approval shall be required for any such law authorizing the creation of a debt or debts in a specified amount or an amount to be determined in accordance with such law for the refinancing of all or a portion of any outstanding debts or liabilities of the State heretofore or hereafter created, so long as such law shall require that the refinancing provide a debt service savings determined in a manner to be provided in such law and that the proceeds of such debt or debts and any investment income therefrom shall be applied to the payment of the principal of, any redemption premium on, and interest due and to become due on such debts or liabilities being refinanced on or prior to the redemption date or maturity date thereof, together with the costs associated with such refinancing. All money to be raised by the authority of such law shall be applied only to the specific object stated therein, and to the payment of the debt thereby created. This paragraph shall not be construed to refer to any money that has been or may be deposited with this State by the government of the United States. Nor shall anything in this paragraph contained apply to the creation of any debts or liabilities for purposes of war, or to repel invasion, or to suppress insurrection or to meet an emergency caused by disaster or act of God.

This paragraph is based on Article IV, section 6, paragraph 4, of the 1844 Constitution. The 1947 Constitution replaced the $100,000 debt limit in the 1844 Constitution with the current 1 percent of appropriations debt limit. The paragraph was amended in 1983 to permit the refinancing of state debt without voter approval if such refinancing would save money.

The purpose of this paragraph is to limit the amount of debt the state government may incur, but to permit additional debts if authorized by law for "some single object or work distinctly specified therein," and approved by the voters, or in the case of war or emergency. The provision therefore requires direct involvement of the voters in most major fiscal indebtedness decisions. Many bond issues have been approved using this mechanism. The reason for a provision like this is to prevent a present legislature from incurring debts that must be paid by future legislatures.

The New Jersey Supreme Court noted the purpose for this limitation in Clayton v. Kervick:

The history of the times renders evident the purpose of the 1844 provision. Early in the 19th Century many of the states borrowed for the development of highways, canals and other internal improvements. Business boomed, money was plentiful, and the states had little difficulty in selling their bonds. By 1840 the bonded indebtedness of the states exceeded the then tidy sum of $200,000,000. However, with the aftermaths of the financial crisis of 1837, the borrowing states found themselves in difficulties and many states defaulted on their bond obligations.

The limitations contained in this paragraph do not apply to political subdivisions such as municipalities and counties (Graziano v. Mayor and Township Committee of Montville). Also, the debts of independent bodies like the Turnpike Authority are not debts of the state and therefore do not fall within the limitations of this paragraph (New Jersey Turnpike Authority v. Parsons). The New Jersey Supreme Court has also held that an independent authority may be created to borrow money and enter into long-term lease agreements for self-liquidating projects, even though this arrangement is intended to circumvent this paragraph (Clayton v. Kervick; New Jersey Sports and Exposition Authority v. McCrane). An anticipated future legislative appropriation for rents on such facilities is not a "debt or liability" within the meaning of this paragraph (Holster v. Passaic Co. College Bd. of Trustees).

The New Jersey Supreme Court has rendered a broad interpretation of the requirement that the law authorizing a debt, on which the voters must express their approval, be limited to a "single object or work." In New Jersey Association on Correction v. Lan, the Court concluded that facilities to be constructed with bonded indebtedness only had to be reasonably related to each other so that voters may understand the proposed projects, and that the legislature could not lump unpopular projects with more popular projects.

> 4. There shall be credited annually to a special account in the General Fund an amount equivalent to the revenue derived from $0.025 per gallon from the tax imposed on the sale of motor fuels pursuant to chapter 39 of Title 54 of the Revised Statutes provided, however, the dedication and use of such revenues as provided in this paragraph shall be subject and subordinate to (a) all appropriations of revenues from such taxes made by laws previously enacted in accordance with Article VIII, Section II, paragraph 3 of the State Constitution in order to provide the ways and means to pay the principal and interest on bonds of the State presently outstanding or authorized to be issued under such laws or (b) any other use of those revenues previously enacted into law. This amount shall be appropriated from time to time by the Legislature, only for the purposes of paying or financing the cost of planning, acquisition, engineering, construction, reconstruction, repair and rehabilitation of the transportation system in this State and it shall not be competent for the Legislature to borrow, appropriate or use this amount or any part thereof for any other purpose, under any pretense whatever. The provisions of this paragraph shall be of no effect after 17 years from the date on which this amendment becomes part of the Constitution.

This paragraph was added to the constitution by amendment in 1984. It dedicates or earmarks a fraction of the gasoline tax, not otherwise obligated under the mechanism provided in paragraph 3, for transportation purposes for the period of seventeen years. This paragraph has not been the subject of judicial interpretation.

SECTION III

> 1. The clearance, replanning, development or redevelopment of blighted areas shall be a public purpose and public use, for which private property may be taken or acquired. Municipal, public or private corporations may be authorized by law to undertake such clearance, replanning, development or redevelopment; and improvements made for these purposes and uses, or for any of them, may be exempted from taxation, in whole or in part, for a limited period of time during which the profits of and dividends payable by any private corporation enjoying such tax exemption shall be limited by law. The conditions of use, ownership, management and control of such improvements shall be regulated by law.

This paragraph, new in the 1947 Constitution, serves several purposes. It indicates that urban redevelopment constitutes a public purpose for which the power of eminent domain may be used (McClintock v. City of Trenton) and creates a specific exception to the rule in Article VIII, Section I, paragraph 2, that tax exemptions may only be granted by general law. It also permits the legislature to delegate to municipalities the power to grant tax exemptions or tax abatements, for limited periods of time, to encourage redevelopment activities. It has not been the subject of judicial interpretation.

> 2. No county, city, borough, town, township or village shall hereafter give any money or property, or loan its money or credit, to or in aid of any individual, association or corporation, or become security for, or be directly or indirectly the owner of, any stock or bonds of any association or corporation.

This paragraph was added by amendment in 1875 and was carried over verbatim in the 1947 Constitution. It, and the next paragraph, are aimed at *local government* indebtedness, as opposed to the earlier limits on *state* debts and lending of credit contained in Article VIII, Section II. Both the state debt and credit limits and the local government limits arose in response to abuses in the financing of railroads and other improvements (Roe v. Kervick).

Challenges to contracts between local governments and private entrepreneurs have been rejected when the courts view the basic purpose of the contracts to further the public interest (Whelan v. New Jersey Power and Light Co.) and when there is consideration (a benefit to the government or citizens) arising from the contract (Bayonne v. Palmer). The courts therefore "have refused to give those provisions a literal reading such as would tie the hands of the government" (In re North Jersey District Water Supply Commission). This paragraph is generally interpreted according to the same constitutional principles limiting the state from lending its credit to private interests (D'Ercole v. Mayor and Council of Norwood), with the basic issue being whether the expenditure furthers the public interest, as that is viewed by the courts over time (Roe v. Kervick).

> 3. No donation of land or appropriation of money shall be made by the State or any county or municipal corporation to or for the use of any society, association or corporation whatever.

This paragraph was also added by amendment in 1875 and was carried over with the addition of the word "county" in the 1947 Constitution. It limits both the state and local governments and is often interpreted together with the preceding paragraph and Article VIII, Section II, paragraph 1 (Roe v. Kervick). Expenditures of government funds to private entities do not violate this provision where they are for a public purpose and the private entity provides a benefit or quid pro quo (Bayonne v. Palmer).

The basic thrust of this and the related provisions is that "public money is used for public purposes" (Township of Mount Laurel v. Department of Public Advocate). The New Jersey Supreme Court has upheld a statute providing that a percentage of horse racing bets be directed to a private horse racing association, on the grounds that these were not public monies (Horsemen's Benevolent and Protective Assoc. v. Atlantic City Racing Assoc.).

SECTION IV

> 1. The Legislature shall provide for the maintenance and support of a thorough and efficient system of free public schools for the instruction of all the children in the State between the ages of five and eighteen years.

This paragraph, added to the 1844 Constitution by amendment in 1875, is often referred to as the "Thorough and Efficient" clause. It mandates a system of free public schools, and, beginning in 1973, formed the constitutional basis for legal challenges to disparities in levels of funding of public education from property taxes in different parts of the state (Robinson v. Cahill [1973]; Abbott v. Burke).[51]

The school finance litigation in New Jersey led the New Jersey Supreme Court to conclude that education is a fundamental right and that it could order the redistribution of state funds appropriated for education (Robinson v. Cahill [1975]). A new round of litigation was begun in the late 1980s (Abbott v. Burke).

With regard to education rights other than unequal funding, the New Jersey Supreme Court has also aggressively enforced the state constitutional right to education. For example, although it concluded that profoundly retarded children classified as "subtrainable" did not have a right to a free education under this paragraph, the Court, referring to the Robinson litigation, stated in Levine v. Department of Institutions and Agencies:

There can be little doubt that the constitutional provision for public education, designed to serve the needs of an enlightened citizenry in a democratic society, was intended by its framers to be expansive in application. . . . The content of the Constitution's education clause is infused with the dynamism inherent in the education process itself. Thus, advances in the field of education, as well as in allied fields such as medical science and human psychology, progressively create opportunities for ever-greater numbers of children, previously impervious to instruction, to become amenable to education.

> 2. The fund for the support of free public schools, and all money, stock and other property, which may hereafter be appropriated for that purpose, or received into the treasury under the provisions of any law heretofore passed to augment the said fund, shall be securely invested, and remain a perpetual fund; and the income thereof, except so much as it may be judged expedient to apply to an increase of the capital, shall be annually appropriated to the support of free public schools, and for the equal benefit of all the people of the State; and it shall not be competent, except as hereinafter provided, for the Legislature to borrow, appropriate or use the said fund or any part thereof for any other purpose, under any pretense whatever. The

bonds of any school district of this State, issued according to law, shall be proper and secure investments for the said fund and, in addition, said fund, including the income therefrom and any other moneys duly appropriated to the support of free public schools may be used in such manner as the Legislature may provide by law to secure the payment of the principal of or interest on bonds or notes issued for school purposes by counties, municipalities or school districts or for the payment or purchase of any such bonds or notes or any claims for interest thereon.

This paragraph dates from Article IV, section 7, paragraph 6, of the 1844 Constitution. It was amended in 1875 to require *free* public schools and in 1958 to permit investment by the fund in bonds of local school districts. This provision limits the legislature to using income from the school fund only for public school purposes by "constitutionalizing" the school fund that, prior to 1844, was provided for by statute. The 1981 amendment creating Section V, paragraph 1, of this Article, removed some riparian (property below the mean high water mark on tidally flowed property) lands from state ownership. Prior to the amendment, the income from such riparian lands had been dedicated to the state school fund by statute. A challenge to the constitutional amendment on the ground that it interfered with the "perpetual" nature of the school fund was rejected because "the people have a right to amend their Constitution" (Dickinson v. Fund for Support of Free Public Schools).

> 3. The Legislature may, within reasonable limitations as to distance to be prescribed, provide for the transportation of children within the ages of five to eighteen years inclusive to and from any school.

This paragraph was added by the 1947 Constitution, to make it clear that the legislature could provide support for transportation of school children attending private (including religious) as well as public schools without offending the establishment of religion provision of Article I, paragraph 4 (West Morris Regional Bd. of Ed. v. Sills). At the time of the 1947 Constitutional Convention, the United States Supreme Court had already upheld a New Jersey school transportation law covering private school students (Everson v. Bd. of Ed. of Ewing Township). The clause prevented any state constitutional challenge to the practice.

SECTION V

> 1. No lands that were formerly tidal flowed, but which have not been tidal flowed at any time for a period of 40 years, shall be deemed riparian lands, or lands subject to a riparian claim, and the passage of that period shall be a good and sufficient bar to any such claim, unless during that period the State has specifically defined and asserted such a claim pursuant to law. This section shall apply to lands which have not been tidal flowed

at any time during the 40 years immediately preceding adoption of this amendment with respect to any claim not specifically defined and asserted by the State within 1 year of the adoption of this amendment.

This paragraph was added to the constitution by amendment in 1981. Prior to the vote on the amendment, the courts ordered a revision of a misleading ballot summary (Gormley v. Lan).

The purpose of the amendment was to eliminate uncertainties to title to tidal properties (the state owns property below the mean high water mark) and to expedite the resolution of title disputes by providing, in effect, a statute of limitations for state claims to lands that have not been tidally flowed for forty years (Dickinson v. Fund for Support of Free Public Schools; City of Jersey City v. Tidelands Resource Council).

Article IX

Amendments

1. Any specific amendment or amendments to this Constitution may be proposed in the Senate or General Assembly. At least twenty calendar days prior to the first vote thereon in the house in which such amendment or amendments are first introduced, the same shall be printed and placed on the desks of the members of each house. Thereafter and prior to such vote a public hearing shall be held thereon. If the proposed amendment or amendments or any of them shall be agreed to by three-fifths of all the members of each of the respective houses, the same shall be submitted to the people. If the same or any of them shall be agreed to by less than three-fifths but nevertheless by a majority of all the members of each of the respective houses, such proposed amendment or amendments shall be referred to the Legislature in the next legislative year; and if in that year the same or any of them shall be agreed to by a majority of all the members of each of the respective houses, then such amendment or amendments shall be submitted to the people.

This article governs the mechanisms for the submission and approval of amendments to the constitutional text. The 1776 Constitution contained no such provisions, and the 1844 version of Article IX set forth a relatively cumbersome set of requirements.

Article IX, as substantially revised in 1947, eliminated some of the rigidity caused by the 1844 section, but state constitutional amendment in New Jersey remains relatively difficult in comparison to a number of other states, such as those permitting constitutional amendments to be put on the ballot by popular initiative.

This initial paragraph is based upon, but includes substantial departures from, the 1844 provision. It includes the requirement of public hearings by the legislature on proposed constitutional amendments. Amendments that receive the support of at least three-fifths of "all of the members of each" house are then submitted to the people for approval or rejection. However, if a proposed constitutional amendment is approved by a majority, but less than three-fifths of the members of each house, it is then "referred to the Legislature in the next legislative year." If, during that next year, the proposed amendment receives at least majority support, it is then submitted to the people (Kimmelman v. Burgio).

Although this paragraph seems to indicate that the only mechanism for constitutional change is by legislative proposal, it is clear that other techniques have been used for the purpose of broader constitutional revision. The 1844 Constitutional Convention, the 1873 Constitutional Commission, which submitted recommended amendments to the legislature, the 1942 Constitutional Commission, and the 1947 and 1966 Constitutional Conventions are good examples of this. As the New Jersey Supreme Court observed in 1964 in Jackman v. Bodine:

Our Constitution . . . is silent as to constitutional conventions, but it is perfectly clear that the Legislature may provide, as it did in 1844 and 1947, the machinery whereby the people can meet in convention through their delegates in pursuit of their "right at all times to alter or reform" the government. Constitution of 1947, Art. I, par. 2.

In 1898 the New Jersey Supreme Court stated in Bott v. Sec. of State:

In every government organized under a constitutional form of government the initial steps for a change in the constitution are with the legislative department of the government in which is vested the sovereign power of the people in that respect.

    2. The proposed amendment or amendments shall be entered on the journal of each house with the yeas and nays of the members voting thereon.

This provision expresses the policy choice that the votes of members of the legislature on proposed constitutional amendments be recorded in the journals. It was included in the 1844 provision. It has not been the subject of judicial interpretation.

    3. The Legislature shall cause the proposed amendment or amendments to be published at least once in one or more newspapers of each county, if any be published therein, not less than three months prior to submission to the people.

This requirement, originating in the 1844 provision, was intended "to disseminate information regarding a proposed constitutional amendment to members of the public."[52] Its provisions would most likely be interpreted to be mandatory, so that failure to publish proposed amendments according to this requirement could lead to a judicial order barring a vote on the proposed amendment, or, even invalidating an amendment apparently ratified by the voters. This paragraph, however, has not been the subject of judicial interpretation.

> 4. The proposed amendment or amendments shall then be submitted to the people at the next general election in the manner and form provided by the Legislature.

Matters concerning the submission of proposed constitutional amendments to the people are governed by Article II, paragraph 2, as well as this paragraph. This provision, based on the 1844 version, except for the general election requirement, leaves to the legislature the question of how to present proposed constitutional amendments to the voters. The legislature has implemented this paragraph, requiring presentation in simple language and with brief interpretive statements. (N.J.S.A. § 19: 3–6 et seq.) The New Jersey courts have been willing to supervise the manner of presentation of proposed constitutional amendments to the voters and to order reformulation of what they conclude to be misleading interpretive statements (Gormley v. Lan; Kimmelman v. Burgio).

> 5. If more than one amendment be submitted, they shall be submitted in such manner and form that the people may vote for or against each amendment separately and distinctly.

This provision, also included in the 1844 version, is obviously intended to permit separate consideration by the voters of distinct proposed amendments. A challenge to an 1897 amendment permitting lotteries, presented with two other proposed amendments, argued unsuccessfully that the voters should, under this provision, be permitted not to vote at all (rather than just for or against) on one or more of the amendments (Bott v. Sec. of State). The requirement contained in this paragraph is enforceable by the courts (Bott v. Sec. of State).

> 6. If the proposed amendment or amendments or any of them shall be approved by a majority of the legally qualified voters of the State voting thereon, the same shall become part of the Constitution on the thirtieth day after the election, unless otherwise provided in the amendment or amendments.

This paragraph governs the effective dates of amendments that are approved by ''a majority of the legally qualified voters of the State voting thereon,'' providing one for those situations where the amendment itself does not contain an effective date. Relying on the words ''voting thereon,'' which were also in the 1844 version, the courts rejected a challenge to the 1897 lottery amendment on the ground that a majority of *all registered voters* had not approved it (Bott v. Sec. of State).

> 7. If at the election a proposed amendment shall not be approved, neither such proposed amendment nor one to effect the same or substantially the same change in the Constitution shall be submitted to the people before the third general election thereafter.

This paragraph, aimed at shielding the voters from a constant resubmission of rejected constitutional amendments, is substantially liberalized from the 1844 version, which stated that "no amendment or amendments shall be submitted to the people by the legislature oftener than once in five years." The issue apparently never arose in New Jersey, but the Pennsylvania Supreme Court interpreted identical language to mean that no proposed amendments of any kind could be submitted to the voters except after at least five-year intervals (Armstrong v. King).

This paragraph was unsuccessfully invoked in an attempt to block the submission of the Atlantic City casino gambling amendment within two years of the defeat at the polls of a proposed *statewide* casino gambling amendment. The Law Division concluded that "although both proposed amendments are concerned with establishing casino gambling in New Jersey, they differ in three significant respects" (Young v. Byrne).

Article X

General Provisions

1. The seal of the State shall be kept by the Governor, or person administering the office of Governor, and used by him officially, and shall be called the Great Seal of the State of New Jersey.

This provision appeared for the first time as Article XI of the 1776 Constitution, providing that "the Council and Assembly shall have power to make the Great Seal of this Colony." It appeared as Article VIII, paragraph 2, of the 1844 Constitution. It was carried over, with only minor editorial changes, in the 1947 Constitution and has not been the subject of judicial interpretation.

2. All grants and commissions shall be in the name and by the authority of the State of New Jersey, sealed with the Great Seal, signed by the Governor, or person administering the office of Governor, and countersigned by the Secretary of State, and shall run thus: "The State of New Jersey, to _____, Greeting."

This paragraph has its origins in Article XV of the 1776 Constitution, which also referred to the "Colony of New Jersey." It was expanded in Article VIII, paragraph 3, of the 1844 Constitution, to read, except for minor editorial changes, as it does today. It governs the form of commissions granted by the governor "to all officers elected or appointed pursuant to this Constitution," pursuant to Article V, Section I, paragraph 12. The paragraph has not been the subject of judicial interpretation.

3. All writs shall be in the name of the State. All indictments shall conclude: "against the peace of this State, the government and dignity of the same."

This paragraph also has its origins in Article XV of the 1776 Constitution. It was, in basically the same language, included in Article VIII, paragraph 3, of the 1844 Constitution, but was relegated to a separate paragraph in the 1947 Constitution.

The provision concerns both "writs" and indictments. Indictments are required in most criminal cases by Article I, paragraph 8. With respect to indictments, the specified language has been held to be only a matter of form, so that indictments that are defective in this respect may be amended (State v. Adamo).

> 4. Wherever in this Constitution the term "person", "persons", "people" or any personal pronoun is used, the same shall be taken to include both sexes.

This paragraph was added by the 1947 Constitutional Convention as part of its attempt to provide equal rights for women. The major component of that modification was to change the word "men" to "persons" in Article I, paragraph 1.[53]

> 5. Except as herein otherwise provided, this Constitution shall take effect on the first day of January in the year of our Lord one thousand nine hundred and forty-eight.

This provides the basic "effective date" for the 1947 Constitution. Article VIII, paragraph 4, of the 1844 Constitution contained a similar provision.

The reference to "Except as herein otherwise provided" relates to the specific phase-in provisions contained in the detailed Schedule—Article XI. Such a detailed schedule is necessary for any new state constitution to phase it into an ongoing, operating system of government.

Article XI

Schedule

This article contains various phase-in provisions designed to facilitate the smooth transition to the 1947 Constitution and several subsequent amendments. Its provisions are self-explanatory and do not have current importance, so the article is reproduced here without section-by-section comment.

SECTION I

1. This Constitution shall supersede the Constitution of one thousand eight hundred and forty-four as amended.

2. The Legislature shall enact all laws necessary to make this Constitution fully effective.

3. All law, statutory and otherwise, all rules and regulations of administrative bodies and all rules of courts in force at the time this Constitution or any Article thereof takes effect shall remain in full force until they expire or are superseded, altered or repealed by this Constitution or otherwise.

4. Except as otherwise provided by this Constitution, all writs, actions, judgments, decrees, causes of action, prosecutions, contracts, claims and rights of individuals and of bodies corporate, and of the State, and all charters and franchises shall continue unaffected notwithstanding the taking effect of any Article of this Constitution.

5. All indictments found before the taking effect of this Constitution or any Article may be proceeded upon. After the taking effect thereof, indict-

ments for crime and complaints for offenses committed prior thereto may be found, made and proceeded upon in the courts having jurisdiction thereof.

SECTION II

1. The first Legislature under this Constitution shall meet on the second Tuesday in January, in the year one thousand nine hundred and forty-eight.

2. Each member of the General Assembly, elected at the election in the year one thousand nine hundred and forty-seven, shall hold office for a term beginning at noon of the second Tuesday in January in the year one thousand nine hundred and forty-eight and ending at noon of the second Tuesday in January in the year one thousand nine hundred and fifty. Each member of the General Assembly elected thereafter shall hold office for the term provided by this Constitution.

3. Each member of the Senate elected in the years one thousand nine hundred and forty-five and one thousand nine hundred and forty-six shall hold office for the term for which he was elected. Each member of the Senate elected in the year one thousand nine hundred and forty-seven shall hold office for a term of four years beginning at noon of the second Tuesday in January following his election. The seats in the Senate which would have been filled in the years hereinafter designated had this Constitution not been adopted shall be filled by election as follows: of those seats which would have been filled by election in the year one thousand nine hundred and forty-eight, three seats, as chosen by the Senate in the year one thousand nine hundred and forty-eight, shall be filled by election in that year for terms of five years, and three, as so chosen, shall be filled by election in that year for terms of three years, and those seats which would have been filled by election in the year one thousand nine hundred and forty-nine shall be filled by election in that year for terms of four years, so that eleven seats in the Senate shall be filled by election in the year one thousand nine hundred and fifty-one and every fourth year thereafter for terms of four years, and the members of the Senate so elected and their successors shall constitute one class to be elected as prescribed in paragraph 2 of Section II of Article IV of this Constitution, and ten seats shall be filled by election in the year one thousand nine hundred and fifty-three and every fourth year thereafter for terms of four years, and the members of the Senate so elected and their successors shall constitute the other class to be elected as prescribed in said paragraph of this Constitution.

4. The provisions of paragraph 1 of Section V of Article IV of this Constitution shall not prohibit the nomination, election or appointment of any member of the Senate or General Assembly first organized under this Constitution, to any State civil office or position created by this Constitution or created during his first term as such member.

SECTION III

1. A Governor shall be elected for a full term at the general election to be held in the year one thousand nine hundred and forty-nine and every fourth year thereafter.

2. The taking effect of this Constitution or any provision thereof shall not of itself affect the tenure, term, status or compensation of any person then holding any public office, position or employment in this State, except as provided in this Constitution. Unless otherwise specifically provided in this Constitution, all constitutional officers in office at the time of its adoption shall continue to exercise the authority of their respective offices during the term for which they shall have been elected or appointed and until the qualification of their successors respectively. Upon the taking effect of this Constitution all officers of the militia shall retain their commissions subject to the provisions of Article V, Section III.

3. The Legislature, in compliance with the provisions of this Constitution, shall prior to the first day of July, one thousand nine hundred and forty-nine, and may from time to time thereafter, allocate by law the executive and administrative offices, departments and instrumentalities of the State government among and within the principal departments. If such allocation shall not have been completed within the time limited, the Governor shall call a special session of the Legislature to which he shall submit a plan or plans for consideration to complete such allocation; and no other matters shall be considered at such session.

SECTION IV

1. Subsequent to the adoption of this Constitution the Governor shall nominate and appoint, with the advice and consent of the Senate, a Chief Justice and six Associate Justices of the new Supreme Court from among the persons then being the Chancellor, the Chief Justice and Associate Justices of the old Supreme Court, the Vice Chancellors and Circuit Court Judges. The remaining judicial officers enumerated and such Judges of the Court of Errors and Appeals as have been admitted to the practice of law in this State for at least ten years, and are in office on the adoption of the Constitution, shall constitute the Judges of the Superior Court. The Justices of the new Supreme Court and the Judges of the Superior Court so designated shall hold office each for the period of his term which remains unexpired at the time the Constitution is adopted; and if reappointed he shall hold office during good behavior. No Justice of the new Supreme Court or Judge of the Superior Court shall hold his office after attaining the age of seventy years, except, however, that such Justice or Judge may complete the period of his term which remains unexpired at the time the Constitution is adopted.

2. The Judges of the Courts of Common Pleas shall constitute the Judges of the County Courts, each for the period of his term which remains unexpired at the time the Judicial Article of this Constitution takes effect.

3. The Court of Errors and Appeals, the present Supreme Court, the Court of Chancery, the Prerogative Court and the Circuit Courts shall be abolished when the Judicial Article of this Constitution takes effect; and all their jurisdiction, functions, powers and duties shall be transferred to and divided between the new Supreme Court and the Superior Court according as jurisdiction is vested in each of them under this Constitution.

4. Except as otherwise provided in this Constitution and until otherwise provided by law, all courts now existing in this State, other than those abolished in paragraph 3 hereof, shall continue as if this Constitution had not been adopted, provided, however, that when the Judicial Article of this Constitution takes effect, the jurisdiction, powers and functions of the Court of Common Pleas, Orphans' Court, Court of Oyer and Terminer, Court of Quarter Sessions and Court of Special Sessions of each county, the judicial officers, clerks and employees thereof, and the causes pending therein and their files, shall be transferred to the County Court of the county. All statutory provisions relating to the county courts aforementioned of each county and to the Judge or Judges thereof shall apply to the new County Court of the county and the Judge or Judges thereof, unless otherwise provided by law. Until otherwise provided by law and except as aforestated, the judicial officers, surrogates and clerks of all courts now existing, other than those abolished in paragraph 3 hereof, and the employees of said officers, clerks, surrogates and courts shall continue in the exercise of their duties, as if this Constitution had not been adopted.

5. The Supreme Court shall make rules governing the administration and practice and procedure of the County Court; and the Chief Justice of the Supreme Court shall be the administrative head of these courts with power to assign any Judge thereof of any county to sit temporarily in the Superior Court or to sit temporarily without the county in a County Court.

6. The Advisory Masters appointed to hear matrimonial proceedings and in office on the adoption of this Constitution shall, each for the period of his term which remains unexpired at the time the Constitution is adopted, continue so to do as Advisory Masters to the Chancery Division of the Superior Court, unless otherwise provided by law.

7. All Special Masters in Chancery, Masters in Chancery, Supreme Court Commissioners and Supreme Court Examiners shall, until otherwise provided by rules of the Supreme Court, continue respectively as Special Masters, Masters, Commissioners and Examiners of the Superior Court, with appropriate similar functions and powers as if this Constitution had not been adopted.

8. When the Judicial Article of this Constitution takes effect:

(a) All causes and proceedings of whatever character pending in the Court of Errors and Appeals shall be transferred to the new Supreme Court;

(b) All causes and proceedings of whatever character pending on appeal or writ of error in the present Supreme Court and in the Prerogative Court and all pending causes involving the prerogative writs shall be transferred to the Appellate Division of the Superior Court;

(c) All causes and proceedings of whatever character pending in the Supreme Court other than those stated shall be transferred to the Superior Court;

(d) All causes and proceedings of whatever character pending in the Prerogative Court other than those stated shall be transferred to the Chancery Division of the Superior Court;

(e) All causes and proceedings of whatever character pending in all other courts which are abolished shall be transferred to the Superior Court;

For the purposes of this paragraph, paragraph 4 and paragraph 9, a cause shall be deemed to be pending notwithstanding that an adjudication has been entered therein, provided the time limited for review has not expired or the adjudication reserves to any party the right to apply for further relief.

9. The files of all causes pending in the Court of Errors and Appeals shall be delivered to the Clerk of the new Supreme Court; and the files of all causes pending in the present Supreme Court, the Court of Chancery and the Prerogative Court shall be delivered to the Clerk of the Superior Court. All other files, books, papers, records and documents and all property of the Court of Errors and Appeals, the present Supreme Court, the Prerogative Court, the Chancellor and the Court of Chancery, or in their custody, shall be disposed of as shall be provided by law.

10. Upon the taking effect of the Judicial Article of this Constitution, all the functions, powers and duties conferred by statute, rules or otherwise upon the Chancellor, the Ordinary, and the Justices and Judges of the courts abolished by this Constitution, to the extent that such functions, powers and duties are not inconsistent with this Constitution, shall be transferred to and may be exercised by Judges of the Superior Court until otherwise provided by law or rules of the new Supreme Court; excepting that such statutory powers not related to the Administration of justice as are then vested in any such judicial officers shall, after the Judicial Article of this Constitution takes effect and until otherwise provided by law, be transferred to and exercised by the Chief Justice of the new Supreme Court.

11. Upon the taking effect of the Judicial Article of this Constitution, the Clerk of the Supreme Court shall become the Clerk of the new Supreme Court and shall serve as such Clerk until the expiration of the term for which

he was appointed as Clerk of the Supreme Court, and all employees of the Supreme Court as previously constituted, of the Clerk thereof and of the Chief Justice and the Justices thereof, of the Circuit Courts and the Judges thereof and of the Court of Errors and Appeals shall be transferred to appropriate similar positions with similar compensation and civil service status under the Clerk of the new Supreme Court or the new Supreme Court, or the Clerk of the Superior Court or the Superior Court, which shall be provided by law.

12. Upon the taking effect of the Judicial Article of this Constitution, the Clerk in Chancery shall become the Clerk of the Superior Court and shall serve as such Clerk until the expiration of the term for which he was appointed as Clerk in Chancery, and all employees of the Clerk in Chancery, the Court of Chancery, the Chancellor and the several Vice Chancellors shall be transferred to appropriate similar positions with similar compensation and civil service status under the Clerk of the Superior Court or the Superior Court, which shall be provided by law.

13. Appropriations made by law for judicial expenditures during the fiscal year one thousand nine hundred and forty-eight, one thousand nine hundred and forty-nine may be transferred to similar objects and purposes required by the Judicial Article.

14. The Judicial Article of this Constitution shall take effect on the fifteenth day of September, one thousand nine hundred and forty-eight, except that the Governor, with the advice and consent of the Senate, shall have the power to fill vacancies arising prior thereto in the new Supreme Court and the Superior Court; and except further that any provision of this Constitution which may require any act to be done prior thereto or in preparation therefor shall take effect immediately upon the adoption of this Constitution.

SECTION V

1. For the purpose of electing senators in 1967 and until the 1970 decennial census of the United States for New Jersey shall have been received by the Governor, the forty senators are hereby allocated among fifteen Senate districts, as follows:

First District—the counties of Gloucester, Atlantic and Cape May, two senators;

Second District—the counties of Salem and Cumberland, one senator;

Third District—the county of Camden, three senators;

Fourth District—the counties of Burlington and Ocean, two senators;

Fifth District—the county of Monmouth, two senators;

Sixth District—the county of Mercer, two senators;

Seventh District—the county of Middlesex, three senators;

Eighth District—the county of Somerset, one senator;

Ninth District—the county of Union, three senators;

Tenth District—the county of Morris, two senators;

Eleventh District—the county of Essex, six senators;

Twelfth District—the county of Hudson, four senators;

Thirteenth District—the county of Bergen, five senators;

Fourteenth District—the county of Passaic, three senators; and

Fifteenth District—the counties of Sussex, Warren and Hunterdon, one senator.

2. For the purpose of electing members of the General Assembly and the senators from Assembly districts where so required in 1967 and until the 1970 census of the United States for New Jersey shall have been received by the Governor, the Assembly districts shall be established by an Apportionment Commission consisting of ten members, five to be appointed by the chairman of the State committee of each of the two political parties whose candidates for Governor receive the largest number of votes at the most recent gubernatorial election. Each State chairman, in making such appointments, shall give due consideration to the representation of the various geographical areas of the State. Such Apportionment Commission shall be appointed no earlier than November 10 nor later than November 15, 1966, and their appointments shall be certified by the Secretary of State on or before December 1, 1966. The Commission, by a majority of the whole number of its members, shall certify the establishment of Assembly districts to the Secretary of State on or before February 1, 1967.

3. If such Apportionment Commission fails so to certify the establishment of Assembly districts to the Secretary of State on or before the date fixed or if prior thereto it determines that it will be unable so to do, it shall so certify to the Chief Justice of the Supreme Court of New Jersey, and he shall appoint an eleventh member of the Commission. Such Commission, by a majority of the whole number of its members, shall within one month after the appointment of such eleventh member certify to the Secretary of State the establishment of Assembly districts.

4. The Assembly districts so established shall be used thereafter for the election of members of the General Assembly and shall remain unaltered until the following decennial census of the United States for New Jersey shall have been received by the Governor.

SECTION VI

When this amendment to the Constitution providing for the abolition of the County Courts takes effect:

(a) All the jurisdiction, functions, powers and duties of the County Court of each county, the judicial officers, clerks, employees thereof, and the causes pending therein, and their files, shall be transferred to the Superior Court. Until otherwise provided by law, the judicial officers, surrogates and clerks of the County Courts and the employees of said officers, clerks, surrogates and courts, shall continue in the exercise of their duties as if this amendment had not been adopted. For the purposes of this paragraph, a cause shall be deemed to be pending notwithstanding that an adjudication has been entered therein, provided the time limited for appeal has not expired or the adjudication reserves any party the right for further relief.

(b) All the functions, powers and duties conferred by the statute, rules or otherwise, upon the judges of the County Courts, shall be transferred to and may be exercised by judges of the Superior Court until otherwise provided by law or rules of the Supreme Court.

(c) Until otherwise provided by law, all county clerks shall become clerks of the Law Division of the Superior Court and all surrogates shall become clerks of the Chancery Division (Probate Part) of the Superior Court for their respective counties and shall perform such duties and maintain such files and records on behalf of the Clerk of the Superior Court as may be required by law and rule of court; and all fees payable to the county clerks and surrogates prior to the effective date of this amendment shall continue to be so payable and be received for the use of their respective counties until otherwise provided by law.

(d) The judges of the County Courts in office on the effective date of this amendment shall be judges of the Superior Court. All such judges who had acquired tenure on a County Court shall hold office as a judge of the Superior Court during good behavior, with all rights, and subject to all the provisions of the Constitution affecting a judge of the Superior Court, as though they were initially appointed to the Superior Court. All other judges of the County Courts shall hold office as judges of the Superior Court, each for the period of his term which remains unexpired on the effective date of this amendment; and if reappointed, he shall hold office during good behavior, with all the rights and subject to all the provisions of the Constitution affecting a judge of the Superior Court as though he were initially appointed to the Superior Court.

Bibliographical Essay

Constitutional development in New Jersey has not generated much commentary. Each of the major stages is covered by one major work, discussed below. The one work that gives a good overview, although it has its major focus on recent constitutional development, is Richard J. Connors, *The Process of Constitutional Revision in New Jersey: 1940–1947* (New York: National Municipal League, 1970). Unfortunately, this book is now out of print.

The following sections will highlight the major sources of information for each stage of New Jersey state constitutional development.

NEW JERSEY COLONIAL CONSTITUTIONAL ANTECEDENTS

Although the colonial antecedents of New Jersey's constitutional development are important, they are beyond the scope of this volume. The most important single work covering constitutional development that includes the colonial charters is Julian R. Boyd, *Fundamental Laws and Constitutions of New Jersey, 1664–1964* (Princeton: D. Van Nostrand Co., 1964). See also William F. Swindler, *Sources and Documents of United States Constitutions* (Dobbs Ferry, N.Y.: Oceana, 1976), 6: 363–472; and Cameron Allen, *A Guide to New Jersey Legal Bibliography and Legal History* (Littleton, Colo.: Fred B. Rothman & Co., 1984), 1–32.

For an excellent set of essays tracing the evolution of the legislative branch, see *The Development of the New Jersey Legislature from Colonial Times to the Present*, William C. Wright, ed. (Trenton: New Jersey Historical Commission, 1979). More recent studies of the colonial legislature are Michael C. Batinski, *The New Jersey Assembly, 1738–1775: The Making of a Legislative Community*

(Lanham, Md.: University Press of America, 1987), and Thomas L. Purvis, *Proprietors, Patronage, and Paper Money: Legislative Politics in New Jersey, 1703–1776* (New Brunswick: Rutgers University Press, 1987).

A good study of the evolution of gubernatorial power, as well as of individual governors, is Duane Lockard, *The New Jersey Governor: A Study in Political Power* (Princeton: Van Nostrand Co., 1964). For bibliographical sketches of each governor, see *The Governors of New Jersey, 1664–1974: Biographical Essays*, Paul A. Stellhorn and Michael J. Birkner, eds. (Trenton: New Jersey Historical Commission, 1982). On the judiciary, see *Jersey Justice: Three Hundred Years of the New Jersey Judiciary*, Carla V. Bello and Arthur J. Vanderbilt, II, eds. (Newark: Institute For Continuing Legal Education, 1978). Alan Shank, *New Jersey Reapportionment Politics: Strategies and Tactics in the Legislative Process* (Rutherford, N.J.: Fairleigh Dickinson University Press, 1969) provides an in-depth, analytical study of apportionment issues from the colonial period to modern times. See also Stanley H. Friedelbaum, "Apportionment Legislation in New Jersey," *Proceedings of the New Jersey Historical Society* 70 (1952):262. Richard P. McCormick traces suffrage issues in *The History of Voting in New Jersey: A Study of the Development of Election Machinery, 1664–1911* (New Brunswick, N.J.: Rutgers University Press, 1953). See also Marion Thompson Wright, "Negro Suffrage in New Jersey, 1776–1875," *Journal of Negro History* 33 (1948):168; J. R. Pole, "The Suffrage in New Jersey, 1790–1807," *Proceedings of the New Jersey Historical Society* 71 (1953):39.

For general treatment of New Jersey's evolution from colony to statehood, see Richard P. McCormick, *New Jersey from Colony to State, 1609–1789* (Newark: New Jersey Historical Society, 1981); Donald M. Kemmerer, *The Path to Freedom: The Struggle for Self-Government in Colonial New Jersey, 1703–1776* (Princeton: Princeton University Press, 1940); Larry R. Gerlach, *Prologue to Independence: New Jersey in the Coming of the American Revolution* (New Brunswick: Rutgers University Press, 1976). An excellent law review treatment is found in Stephen Presser, "An Introduction to the Legal History of Colonial New Jersey," *Rutgers-Camden Law Journal* 7 (1976):262.

THE 1776 CONSTITUTION

The definitive work on the 1776 Constitution, although it is now out of print, is Charles Erdman, Jr., *The New Jersey Constitution of 1776* (Princeton: Princeton University Press, 1929). This work also contains coverage of the criticisms of, and efforts to change, the 1776 Constitution, as well as some of the early judicial interpretation of New Jersey's first constitution. A good summary, in short booklet form, is Richard J. Connors, *The Constitution of 1776* (Trenton: New Jersey Historical Commission, 1975). See also L.Q.C. Elmer, "History of the Constitution of New Jersey, Adopted in 1776," *Proceedings of the New Jersey Historical Society* 2 (1870) (Second Series): 135. The official, although scant, record is contained in *Journal of the Votes and Proceedings of the Convention of New Jersey* (Burlington, 1776).

Larry R. Gerlach edited a very good set of documents reflecting a range of issues during the revolutionary period. *New Jersey in the American Revolution, 1763–1783: A Documentary History* (Trenton: New Jersey Historical Commission, 1975). For in-depth coverage of revolutionary period issues from the point of view of leading individual participants, see John E. O'Connor, *William Patterson: Lawyer and Statesman, 1745–1806* (New Brunswick: Rutgers University Press, 1979), and Ruth Bogin, *Abraham Clark and the Quest for Equality in the Revolutionary Era, 1774–1794* (Rutherford, N.J.: Fairleigh Dickinson University Press, 1982).

The broader questions of state constitutional development in all the states during the revolutionary era are ably treated in Willi Paul Adams, *The First American Constitutions: Republican Ideology and the Making of the State Constitutions in the Revolutionary Era* (Chapel Hill: University of North Carolina Press, 1980), and Donald S. Lutz, *Popular Consent and Popular Control: Whig Political Theory in the Early State Constitutions* (Baton Rouge: Louisiana State University Press, 1980). State constitutional change in the 1820s, outside of New Jersey, is covered in Merrill Peterson, *Democracy, Liberty and Property: The State Constitutional Conventions of the 1820's* (Indianapolis: Bobbs-Merrill, 1966).

For coverage of political developments in New Jersey in the early nineteenth century, see Herbert Ershkowitz, *The Origins of the Whig and Democratic Parties: New Jersey Politics, 1820–1837* (Washington, D.C.: University Press of America, 1982). See also Walter R. Fee, *The Transition from Aristocracy to Democracy in New Jersey, 1789–1829* (Somerville, N.J.: Somerset Press, Inc., 1933); Peter D. Levine, "The Rise of Mass Parties and the Problem of Organization: New Jersey, 1829–1844," *New Jersey History* 91 (Summer 1973):91; Peter D. Levine, *The Behavior of State Legislative Parties in the Jacksonian Era: New Jersey, 1829–1844* (Rutherford, N.J.: Fairleigh Dickinson University Press, 1977); and *Jacksonian New Jersey*, Paul A. Stellhorn, ed. (Trenton: New Jersey Historical Commission, 1979).

THE 1844 CONSTITUTION

New Jersey's 1844 Constitution is the subject of a very good single volume produced by the Federal Writers' Project in 1942. In *Proceedings of the New Jersey State Constitutional Convention of 1844* (Trenton, New Jersey State House Commission, 1942), John Bebout provides a lengthy, analytical introduction, and then collects the "transcripts," which are actually stenographic reporters' notes of the debates that were published daily in newspapers during the 1844 Convention. The volume also includes biographical sketches of the convention delegates. Frederick M. Herrmann gives very good treatment to the events leading to the 1844 Constitution, as well as events immediately following its adoption in "The Constitution of 1844 and Political Change in Antebellum New Jersey," *New Jersey History* 101 (Spring/Summer 1983):29. A much earlier and shorter summary of the 1844 Convention is Francis J. Swayze, "Epitome of the Constitutional Convention of 1844," *Proceedings of the New Jersey Historical Society* 6 (April 1921) (New Series):66.

THE 1873 CONSTITUTIONAL COMMISSION

There is no book-length study, or even an article, about the 1873 Constitutional Commission, which led to a major package of twenty-eight amendments being adopted in 1875. The original, handwritten *Record of Proceedings of the 1873 Constitutional Commission* can be found in the Archives at the State Library in Trenton. Contemporary newspapers carried in-depth coverage of the Commission's work, but there is no collection of these materials. The work of the Commission is briefly summarized in a postscript in John Bebout's introduction to the 1844 *Proceedings*, in Bennett M. Rich, *The Government and Administration of New Jersey* (New York: Thomas Crowell Co., 1957), 18–19, and in Richard J. Connors, *The Process of Constitutional Revision in New Jersey: 1940–1947* (New York: National Municipal League, 1970), 11–13.

1940–1944 CONSTITUTIONAL DEVELOPMENTS

Record of the Proceedings before the Joint Committee of the New Jersey Legislature Constituted Under Senate Concurrent Resolution No. 19 (1942) includes the record of public hearings as well as the 1942 Hendrickson Commission report and its draft constitution. The Commission's proposals are treated in William Miller, "The Report of New Jersey's Constitutional Commission," *American Political Science Review* 36 (1942):900. For Governor Walter E. Edge's personal account of this period of attempted constitutional change, see Walter E. Edge, *A Jerseyman's Journal* (Princeton, N.J.: Princeton University Press, 1948), 258–95.

The proposed 1944 Constitution is found in *Laws of New Jersey, 1944*, chapter 92, pp. 195–241.

THE 1947 CONSTITUTION

The definitive work on the 1947 Constitution, including an excellent summary of New Jersey constitutional development up to that point, is Richard J. Connors, *The Process of Constitutional Revision*. This work also contains excellent biographical notes. Another good treatment is contained in Richard N. Baisden, *Charter for New Jersey: The New Jersey Constitutional Convention of 1947* (Trenton, N.J.: New Jersey Department of Education, 1952). The author served as a staff person during the 1947 Convention. For an anecdotal account of the 1947 Convention by a delegate from Hudson County, see Frank G. Schlosser,

Dry Revolution: Diary of a Constitutional Convention (Newton, 1960). Eugene C. Gerhart, *Arthur T. Vanderbilt: The Compleat Counsellor* (Albany, N.Y.: Q Corporation, 1980), provides a full treatment of Vanderbilt's career, with chapters on his role in constitutional revision in the 1940s, including excerpts from his private correspondence. The November 19, 1987, *New Jersey Law Journal* contains a number of articles commemorating the fortieth anniversary of the 1947 Constitution.

The five-volume State of New Jersey, *Constitutional Convention of 1947* contains a wealth of information concerning New Jersey constitutional development. The set includes a rich set of background papers prepared before the Convention met, as well as transcripts of hearings before the Committees and the floor debates. Leon S. Milmed, "The New Jersey Constitution of 1947," in *New Jersey Statutes Annotated* (St. Paul, Minn.: West Publishing Co., 1971), 1:91–114, contains a review of the changes accomplished by the 1947 Constitution. Milmed, later a judge, had been a legal advisor to the 1947 Constitutional Convention and Counsel to Governor Alfred E. Driscoll. There is an Oral History Project concerning the 1947 Constitutional Convention under way at Rutgers Law School in Newark, under the supervision of Professor Robert A. Carter. For a description of the Project see Robert A. Carter, "Meese, Brennan & Jersey judicial activism," *New Jersey Lawyer* 120 (August 1987):27.

For specific focus on the 1947 Judiciary Article, see Voorhees E. Dunn, Jr., "The Road to the 1947 New Jersey Constitution: Arthur T. Vanderbilt's Influence on Court Reform, 1930–47," *New Jersey History* 104 (Fall/Winter 1986):23. William W. Evans traced the history of court reform proposals from the nineteenth century in "Constitutional Court Reform in New Jersey," *University of Newark Law Review* 7 (1941):1. Excellent coverage of the evolution of the court system, with an analysis of the first forty years of the New Jersey Supreme Court's work, is found in G. Alan Tarr and Mary Cornelia Aldis Porter, *State Supreme Courts in State and Nation* (New Haven: Yale University Press, 1988), 184–236. For another good treatment, see Stanley H. Friedelbaum, "Constitutional Law and Judicial Policy Making," in Richard Lehne and Alan Rosenthal, eds., *Politics in New Jersey*, rev. ed. (New Brunswick: Rutgers University Press, 1979). The volume superceded Rich, *The Government and Administration of New Jersey*. There is, however, a still more recent volume, edited by Gerald M. Pomper, *The Political State of New Jersey* (New Brunswick, N.J.: Rutgers University Press, 1986). This volume contains an excellent chapter on the state court system by John C. Pittenger. In-depth coverage of the New Jersey Supreme Court's involvement with school financing is provided in Richard Lehne, *The Quest for Justice* (New York: Longman, 1978).

NEW JERSEY CONSTITUTIONAL INTERPRETATION

No attempt is made here to list the wide variety of articles about New Jersey constitutional interpretation that have appeared in the New Jersey Law reviews over the years. *Rutgers Law Journal* (Camden); *Rutgers Law Review* (Newark); and *Seton Hall Law Review* contain a wealth of material both on specific judicial opinions interpreting the New Jersey Constitution, as well as articles treating different areas of New Jersey state constitutional law. The reader is referred to the indexes for each of these law reviews, as well as to the materials cited in the notes of this book. Useful articles are also found in the journal of the New Jersey State Bar Association, *New Jersey Lawyer*, and in New Jersey's weekly legal newspaper, the *New Jersey Law Journal*. A recent but relatively incomplete bibliography may be found in *Constitutions of the States: A State By State Guide and Bibliography to Current Scholarly Research*, Bernard D. Reams, Jr., and Stuart D. Yoak, eds. (Dobbs Ferry, N.Y.: Oceana, 1988), 237–43.

A good study of the amendment process under the current constitution, together with successful and unsuccessful amendments through 1962, is Lawrence R. Caruso, "The Amending Process Under the New Jersey Constitution of 1947," *University of Detroit Law Journal* 41 (1964):262. Proposed amendments, including both those rejected and adopted, can be traced up through the present in the current, annual *New Jersey Legislative Manual*.

Research into the interpretation of any specific New Jersey Constitutional provision may be undertaken by checking the "annotations" (summaries of judicial decisions) contained in the first two volumes of the *New Jersey Statutes Annotated*, published by West Publishing Company, St. Paul, Minnesota, and then reading the decisions themselves. Also, modern computerized legal research sources may be used to do New Jersey Constitutional research. These techniques were used to prepare the section-by-section analysis in this book.

Table of Cases

Index

About the Author

ROBERT F. WILLIAMS is Professor of Law at Rutgers Law School. He is the editor of *State Constitutional Law: Cases and Materials*, the first law and political science coursebook on the subject. In addition, he has written, lectured, and practiced widely in the area of state constitutional law.